Begin to Live

DR. HELEN ROSE

ST. MARTIN'S PRESS/NEW YORK

Copyright © 1979 by Helen Rose
All rights reserved. For information, write:
St. Martin's Press, Inc., 175 Fifth Ave., New York, N.Y. 10010.
Manufactured in the United States of America

Library of Congress Cataloging in Publication Data

Rose, Helen.
  Begin to live.

  1. Success. I. Title
BF637.S8R587 1979   158'.1   79-16528
ISBN 0-312-07169-8

This book is lovingly dedicated to Tracy and Bradley.

Never give up!
No matter how old you are,
a good attitude is the most
priceless possession you can have—
an appreciation of life
and what life has to offer.

Dr. Helen Rose

Contents

Introduction		1
1	How to Improve Your Psychological Health	5
2	How to Have More Energy and Vitality	31
3	How to Retard Aging	53
4	How to Improve Your Physical Health	70
5	How to Handle Problems with Your Family	92
6	Divorce in the Later Years	117
7	How to Handle Loneliness	127
8	How to Improve Your Sex Life	142
9	How to Live with a Retired Husband	165
10	How to Heal Psychological Wounds	176
11	It's Time to Live a New Life	180

Introduction

This is a happy book—full of hope, courage, and inspiration. It is written for those people who want to live longer but are afraid of growing older.

We are living in a wonderful time. Scientists tell us that there is no reason why we cannot live to be a hundred. We have to take care of our minds and bodies. The mind has a way of talking to the body and the body talks back with illness.

This book can add years to your life, and show you the way to optimum health, both physically and psychologically.

Now is the time to "live it up." You may have had a terrible childhood, you may be in a bad marriage, you may be widowed or divorced, you may have had lots of unpleasantness in your life. I don't know what you have suffered, but I do know this—you *can* make the rest of your life glorious—so glorious that it will wipe out the unpleasantness in the first part of your life.

This book is about getting younger as you get older. It is for those who prefer to "live" rather than vegetate.

Anyone of any age can benefit from this book—whether you want better health, more energy, a better marriage, a better sex life, more self-confidence, peace of mind, or simply to learn how to take off weight and keep it off without suffering frustration. All of these are realistic goals and can be achieved.

Primarily the book is written for people past fifty. It is then when we become aware of "aging." Don't despair. Scientists tell us that you can do a great deal to retard aging. You can slow down the aging process by positive emotions, right thinking, good nutrition, exercise, and involvement in life. I am addicted to all of these. Those who know me know that I practice what I preach. I feel younger and am healthier today in my fifties, in all the ways that matter, than I was twenty-five years younger.

Most of us say we want to stay young. But, actually, we permit ourselves to be old. When it comes to working at the job of staying youthful (as we grow older), we lose the driving curiosity, the urgent hunger for experiment and adventure, and run for the house slippers and the easy chair.

There is much more to a person than the physical self. There is also the psychological self. This part of us feeds on praise, recognition, and achievement. It thrives on gratification.

Wrong attitudes toward aging are damaging to a person's feelings about himself. It is important to all of us to change our negative attitudes about aging. How you feel about yourself as you get older, and your general attitude toward life and aging are most influential in determining how quickly or slowly you will age. *You* are in control of the aging process. You may not have control over the calendar years—your chronological age—but you do have control over your biological age. Age depends on how well you take care of your body and how well it functions. If you take care of your body, eat properly, learn how to relax and release tension, exercise (even if it is just walking), and learn to deal with stress and anger constructively, you can stay youthful for a long time.

The body has a remarkable ability to regenerate itself. I know some people who have a chronological age of thirty and a biological age of fifty. They have been giving their bodies a beating for years with the food they eat, the thoughts they think, and especially their negative emotions. They can't control anger, they worry a lot, they can't take frustration—they are a mess. They have all kinds of psychosomatic illnesses plus some real medical disorders. On the other hand, I know some people of seventy who biologically are like fifty. They control their emotions, they eat right, they don't smoke, they deal with their problems as they arise, they have positive attitudes. They are in love with life and they look and feel terrific.

The best measure of age, however, is our psychological age—*how old we feel*. Many of us are chained to habits and beliefs that are making us miserable and destroying our health.

If you believe that the best of life is over, it is. You will just be marking time. Here on Miami Beach, where I live, I have heard many people refer to various areas of Florida as "God's Waiting Room." But I have also heard people say that Florida is a Shangri La. These people are living it up every day and are truly involved. They are not marking time. Florida is like any other part of the country: "God's Waiting Room" is an attitude, a negative attitude. A person with this kind of belief does nothing. He stops growing and begins to deteriorate.

If, on the other hand, you look upon the second or third part of your lifetime as a new beginning, it can be a rewarding adventure. Your viewpoint on growing older can either brighten or dim the rest of your years.

The law of life is: Use it or lose it. Underactivity may wear us out from disuse. This applies to our physical, sexual, intellectual, and psychological functioning.

You can start being young again the moment you choose to or you can let go and permit yourself to go downhill. It's no wonder that many people approaching fifty or sixty develop anxieties or depression—they can't believe that anything exciting or worthwhile can happen to them past sixty or seventy. Well, you don't have to dry up just because you are getting older. You can have a meaningful life at any age. Don't listen to people who tell you you're through. You can have another chance at fulfillment. This book tells you how to do it—from one who has done it and is still doing it.

This is the time of life when we need to be even more courageous and optimistic than we were in our earlier years. We must believe that each day is a new day with new opportunities and that no matter what happened yesterday, we *do* get a second, third, and many more chances in life for happiness and fulfillment.

When you finish reading my book you may not be the same person. I hope you will feel like doing a lot more about staying young and living it up. I offer "tools" to repair worn-out marriages and tools to deal effectively with anger, stress, worry, and tension. I tell you how to develop the kind of beauty (no matter how old you are) that no Hollywood makeup man could ever create, because it is an inner beauty that is profound and lasting, which no cream or soap could wash off. You will look better, feel better, live better. You will begin to believe that life *can* be wonderful past fifty, sixty, seventy, and beyond.

Am I promising too much? I would not say this if I had not seen it happen to my students. As a full-time psychology instructor in adult education in Miami, Florida, I have taught approximately thirty thousand students over a period of seven years. It is most rewarding to see my students, whose ages range from fifty to ninety, looking younger than when they first came to my class, full of vigor and vitality, and beginning to live it up.

From the knowledge I have gained from research in the fields of psychology, gerontology, and nutrition; my professional training as a psychotherapist and marriage and family counselor; and through dealing with people over the years in a professional capacity, I am convinced that it *is* possible to stay youthful as we get older, and be happy, in spite of the fact that we may have problems.

Never let the words, "I am getting old," come from your lips. Let's all stay "ageless" together.

How to Improve Your Psychological Health

1

Our attitudes and emotions can make us look much older than we really are. Nothing ages a person faster than negative attitudes and negative emotions. It's no big deal to be unhappy; anyone can be unhappy. To be happy in spite of your problems—that's a big deal. When we think in terms of health, we have to consider our *psychological* health, also. We all know some people who do not have an organic disease or any kind of medical disorder, and yet are very unhappy. They are constantly tense, feel blue or sad, complain, or are just plain miserable. Can we say that these people are healthy? I'm not talking about the occasional blues or a necessary complaint, I'm talking about chronic unhappiness. Unhappiness affects the body chemistry. It lowers body resistance and makes you more susceptible to disease, and it plays havoc with your nervous system. *Chronic unhappiness is a waste of one's life.*

ARE YOU HAPPY?

I know some people who cry, "If only certain things in my life would change, I could be so happy." What is it that changes things? Wishes or action? How can things change when all these people do is merely sit down and *wish* them to change?

There was a time when my own life seemed to be unbelievably difficult. When I became aware that all my difficulties were of my own making, that it was *I*—not other people, not external events, not the outside world—who was making my life unhappy, I worked on my attitudes first. Then I went to work to change what I could change and began to think differently about that which I could not change, and gradually the burdens that seemed so heavy melted away.

Do not consider yourself a victim of circumstance. If you want to improve your life, you may have to change some of the attitudes and/or values that are impeding your happiness. I know of no other way to begin a new life.

Susan, a divorcée of fifty-five, was sent to me by a former client. She had nice features and a slender figure, but she looked tired, almost haggard. I asked her if she got enough sleep. "I wake up tired no matter how much sleep I get," she said. I then asked her if she had had a physical examination recently. Yes, she had. The doctor found nothing physically wrong. In fact, she had gone to two physicians and got the same answer. She wanted to know why she was so drained of energy. As she began to talk the reason became clear. She was beset by fears and anxieties about her future—she felt very insecure without a husband. She had been awarded a reasonable divorce settlement, so she didn't have to worry about any financial problems, but she felt she had nothing to look forward to. She was still suffering from rejection—her husband, fifty-eight, had left her for a woman of sixty.

She could understand it, she said, if he had left her for a younger woman, but an *older* woman was too much! Susan didn't make friends easily, which compounded her agony. She was rather timid and thought of herself as a misfit. She felt she didn't belong with married couples and felt uncomfortable with single people. She was caught in a grip of misery and saw no way out.

I helped Susan to understand that her situation would not change without her putting forth some effort. If her life was to be better, she was the one to make it so. No one has enough emotional strength to live in the past and, at the same time, enough strength to live in the present and create a new life. It is like trying to save a drowning person who is determined to drown. Susan also became aware that unhappiness is self-caused and results from unhealthy and unrealistic thinking, and the inability to tolerate frustration and rejection. When she first came to see me her attitude was in effect that life "owed" you happiness. She soon learned that life owes you *nothing*. All life can give you is the *opportunity* to find your own happiness, to do something with yourself, to improve yourself, to go forward.

Before long, Susan began to feel better. When her drawn look disappeared, she was quite attractive. She learned to think differently, to approach her problems from a new standpoint. She was willing to pay the price for a new life —and life took on a fresh meaning for her.

Do *you* believe that because you have problems you can't smile, that life is terrible? Perhaps some of you do. If you were to believe otherwise—that life is wonderful—you would be able to laugh at a joke, enjoy a good meal or movie or play, in spite of your problems. Then, even if other people or circumstances put restrictions before you, frustrated you, rejected you, they could not make you miserable if you refused to be miserable. If you believe life is wonderful, then you *will* become healthier and happier as you grow older.

Real happiness is so simple that most people do not recognize it. It derives from the most common, unpretentious things in the world—little kindnesses, pleasant words, encouragement, work that we enjoy, friendship, love, and affection. All these are simple things, yet they are what constitute happiness. We cannot equate happiness with material possessions. We have all heard the remark, "He has so much money but he can't enjoy it." I am not negating comfort—material things, luxuries, can *contribute* to happy living—but this happiness is short-lived if we are faced with an overwhelming frustration or disappointment or tragedy and don't have the ability to cope. Coping ability and good attitudes are the *richest* possessions anyone can have. When you feel that you can lick anything—that it won't lick you—this is coping, this is power. What an exhilarating feeling!

Robert, a strong, sturdy, self-made man, is a good example of a person who equated happiness with material things. Not so long ago he was a very rich man. When he came to see me he had lost practically everything. He was a genius at making money, but he knew nothing about the art of living. He suffered from an inner discontent that no amount of money could allay—greed. He was forever unsatisfied.

In our counseling session, he told me that for the first time in his life he had made some foolish investments and had lost practically all his wealth. The result was frustration, conflict, and self-hate. His acute mental suffering had led to heavy drinking. "I know I'm drinking too much," he said. "I've got to get hold of myself or I'll drown." At first, I suggested Alcoholics Anonymous, but he wouldn't hear of it. He felt disgraced enough, he said. His wife had left him just before he lost his wealth because, as he put it, "I was never a husband, I was never home. She didn't have a life with me so she walked out." This, too, added to his self-hate. Nothing seemed to awaken Robert's interest in life again. He could not forgive himself for having made a "mistake." He succumbed to defeat. He was fifty-two years old and considered himself a failure. Robert did not understand that one can fail and yet not be a *failure*. True, his mistake was costly, but the psychological and physical damage he was doing to himself was *more* costly.

Prior to losing his wealth, he had all the things that supposedly make people happy. He lived in a palatial home surrounded by luxuries, and yet the moment misfortune came, what he had called happiness fled. If he had been happy within himself, his misfortune could not have shaken him up as it did. Real happiness is not superficial. It does not live in things.

I gave Robert this assignment:

- Since he couldn't take frustration "straight" he was to try a cocktail with the following ingredients:
    An ounce of constructive thoughts;
    A half-ounce of enthusiasm;
    A half-ounce of optimism.
    He was to drink this cocktail a few times a day. There would be no hangover, because the only thing that could happen to him would be that he would become intoxicated with life. Robert laughed about the cocktail—said he couldn't find it in a liquor store. Of course not—it's just a mental attitude. But I gave him more homework:
- He had to learn to walk away mentally from the past. It no longer exists—it's gone, over, finished. Learn from mistakes and then close the door on them.
- He had to learn to believe in himself again. Until he changed his thinking, he was not going to get anywhere. Everything starts in the mind, and so he was to convince himself that he was indestructible, indomitable, and

invincible. He was to repeat this over and over again until he *believed* it. When you believe something strongly, it goes into the unconscious part of your mind and once the unconscious believes it, a change is produced within you. This kind of attitude would help to alleviate mental suffering and alcohol would no longer be necessary to deaden the emotional pain.
- He had to convince himself that he was not too old to start over again. He could make it again with the *right kind of attitude.*
- He was to keep this little Scottish ballad in his wallet, to look at should he suffer a setback at any time.

> "I am hurt," Sir Andrew Barton said,
> "I am hurt but I am not slain;
> I'll lay me down and bleed a while,
> And then I'll fight again."

- Finally, he had to accept himself as an imperfect human being capable of making mistakes and to forgive himself, not punish himself, if he blundered from time to time.

A few months later he came to see me with his wife, a lovely woman of fifty with eyes that danced with responsiveness. He was a changed man. He had done his "homework." He had started a new business with the help of a friend. He was full of vitality and enthusiasm. "Hey," he said, "you know that cocktail you suggested—it sure beats hard liquor. I'm so high on life. Life is just wonderful!" And he put his arm around his wife and walked out. Robert found his medicine not in the form of alcoholism but in the form of constructive thinking plus constructive action.

EMOTIONAL NOURISHMENT

A word spoken in due season, how good it is.
                                     Proverbs 15:23

There's magic in emotional nourishment, whether we get it from others or give it to ourselves. No matter how old we are, all of us desire affection, approval, acceptance, and encouragement. I desire it, you desire it. Why not? It feels delightful. But when I do not get it, I function very well without it, and so can you—if you *believe* that you can.

The psychological self thrives on gratification and "applause," but many of us don't always get it from others (even from those whom we love). So what do we do? We must nurture ourselves.

The movie, *A Touch of Class,* with George Segal and Glenda Jackson, illustrates this need for applause—in this case, in the bedroom. After they finally "made it" in bed, George asks Glenda, "How was it for you?" Translated, he was really asking, "How was *I?*" Glenda, without too much emotion, responds, "It was okay." *"Okay?!* Is that all you can say?!" George shouts and continues to rant and rave because of the lack of applause from Glenda. What he wanted to hear was, "You were simply terrific—the earth rocked for me—you were fantastic, etc." I need not go into the rest of the movie (he got enough "emotional nourishment" after that scene); my point is that when he didn't get the applause he *needed* he was devastated. It's obvious he doubted his sexual ability. This happens in real life, too—with young men and older men. (More about sex in Chapter 8).

Mark Twain once remarked, "I can live on a good compliment for three weeks." Don't you feel "high" when *you* receive praise? That's real emotional nourishment. With big doses of encouragement, a person's life can be transformed.

Surround yourself with people who have this wonderful quality of nurturing. They are positive thinkers. They build you up—they give you a psychological shot in the arm when you're with them. They are genuinely interested in you, and when you walk away you feel good and uplifted. Stay away from people who tear you down and belittle you, who say to you constantly, "What do you know? You don't know what you're talking about," or, "You say such stupid things, you really should keep your mouth closed." These kinds of remarks, if repeated often enough, tend to inhibit you more and more in social situations and, also, may have a bad effect on your self-image. When I was studying at Columbia University, one of my psychology professors told us something I have never forgotten: As you tell a child he is, so he will become, if you tell it to him often enough.

- "You're such a good little boy/girl."
- "You're so smart."
- "You're so pretty."
- "You're going to do great things someday."

Sigmund Freud attributed his success to his mother's repeated suggestion: "Someday you will be great; I believe in you." Freud internalized his mother's repeated suggestion, which helped to spur him on to become great. This concept also applies to adults. As you tell a person he is, so he will become, if you tell it to him often enough:

- "You're so thoughtful."
- "You're so considerate."
- "You're so generous."
- "You're so good to me."

However, there has to be a kernel of truth in the suggestion. My point is, when you find a person who is thoughtful and considerate sometimes, but not as often as you would like, keep telling the person in different ways how thoughtful and considerate he or she is. The more you tell him, the more he will respond the way you would like him to. You may say, "Oh, but that's like brainwashing." So what? Is it better to brainwash a person with negative suggestions such as:

- "You're so inconsiderate."
- "You're so rotten."
- "You're so stupid."
- "You're a real bastard."

We are all brainwashed to a large extent. Brainwashing goes on all the time. To nurture someone into believing that he is good, thoughtful, strong, and capable of coping with anything is the most beneficial force human beings can use on one another.

Emerson once said: "What I most need is somebody to make me do what I can." Everybody responds to positive suggestion. However, let's remember, *suggestion must be honest and sincere.* If a person can do something but does not do it, it may be a lack of confidence in himself that is holding him back. We can encourage him, nurture him, by telling him that he can do it, that we have faith in him. If the encouragement is repeated often enough, the person feels nurtured enough to do that which he fears to do.

However, if we know for certain that an individual cannot do a particular thing, we should not tell him that he can. If we visit an individual in a hospital who is recuperating from a serious operation and we tell him that he looks terrific (when he really doesn't), not only will the individual disbelieve us, but he will lose confidence in our truthfulness as well. For example, one of my new students, Beatrice, visited a relative in the hospital. On the way to the hospital she decided she would "nourish" her relative to make her feel better. But (as was discussed in class afterward) she didn't realize that she used the wrong kind of suggestion. She burst into the room with: "You look terrific! I'm surprised to see you looking so good." Now this patient really looked bad. The nurse had brought her a mirror earlier to help her comb her hair and the patient saw for herself how bad she looked. It was understandable—she had just gone through an operation and was now recuperating. She said to Beatrice, "Stop the phoniness, I know I look awful." Beatrice felt embarrassed. Had she said something like, "You will be out of here sooner than you think. You will get well soon. You love life. You have a lot to live for," the patient would have felt inspired. This kind of suggestion is nourishing. It gives the patient hope—it cultivates the will to live.

There is nothing insincere about encouraging people when we mean it. It's not "flattery." It's inspiring and beautiful. There are so many discouraged hearts everywhere hungry for a word of affection, for encouragement, waiting to be lifted and strengthened. Many of my students complain: "Not only does my husband not notice my new hairdo or the new dress I'm wearing, but he never says anything about the delicious meals I serve him. I might as well serve him hay for all he notices." Petite Alice, with a beautiful head of dark curly hair, did just that. When her husband, who is retired, came home after playing cards all afternoon and sat down at the dinner table, she served him a heaping pile of hay on a beautiful dinner plate. When he indignantly demanded whether she had gone crazy, she replied, "How did I know you would notice? I have been cooking for you for the past thirty years and in all that time you never said one word to let me know that you *weren't eating hay.*"

Ronald, a retired businessman, told me, "I give my wife everything. I have never denied her a thing and yet she complains that I don't love her. I don't understand it." He *has* denied her something—something vital and essential to human happiness—*emotional nourishment.* Ronald was always a good provider, a good man basically, but could never express love or nurture anyone. In talking with me he admitted he never complimented his wife or praised her, never said anything to her that would make her *feel* loved. Her heart was starving in the midst of luxuries. For example, she wanted him to say the three little words, "I love you." He couldn't say it.

Unfortunately, Ronald had never heard those words in his home as a child. His parents had never shown him love; they had never praised him in any way. How could he give love if he was never given love? He confessed that he had made up his mind in his youth to become so successful that everybody he came in contact with would admire him—he would "fix" his parents.

We spent many hours discussing Ronald's problem, and gradually he realized that you give but little when you give of your possessions. It is when you give of yourself that you truly give. The words "I love you" were difficult for him to say at first, but gradually he was able to say them. Not only to his wife, but also to his grown children and grandchildren. Ronald also began to praise his wife more whenever the opportunity presented itself. In fact, he *looked* for opportunities to express love other than with material things. And soon Ronald began to receive far more warmth and affection from his family, the likes of which he had never experienced.

Try not to be the kind of person who gives out a little emotional nourishment and takes it away at the same time: "I love you, but you're too fat." (If the person were nurtured a little more, he or she would not have to eat so much.) "You're a terrific cook—but you sure mess up dinner parties." "You're a lovely person—but I wish you would get rid of that awful habit." "You're a terrific guy, but . . ." I'm not saying we shouldn't indicate it when something has to be corrected or improved upon. However, when you are giving someone emotional nourishment at a particular time, *simply give it—don't also take it away.* Correct the person or

15

point out the mistake or situation that has to be improved upon at another time.

- "I love you, honey." Period. At another time when the opportunity presents itself: "Darling, you would feel so much better if you lose some weight. You wouldn't be bothered with heartburn."
- "You're a terrific guy." Period. At another time when you and your husband are dressing to visit friends: "John, dear, I think you are unaware that you bite your nails when you get excited during a stimulating conversation. It's no big deal—just be aware of it and gradually you'll break the habit."

THE KIND OF MEDICINE THAT CANNOT BE BOUGHT

The kind of medicine that most people need cannot be bought in a drug store—because we all have this incredible, powerful "medicine" within us. It is in the form of autosuggestion. So far I have been talking about receiving nourishment from others (heterosuggestion), but as I stated earlier, we don't always get the nourishment we need from others, so we must nurture ourselves—through autosuggestion. Many of us *have* to do this, in fact, if more people nourished *themselves* psychologically, there would be happier and healthier people in this world. There would be less illness, fewer feelings of inferiority, and more achievements.

We constantly use autosuggestion unknowingly. Thinking is a form of talking to yourself, too. However, many of us do *not* nurture ourselves—we engage in negative autosuggestion without realizing it. Instead of nurturing ourselves—accepting ourselves with all our faults and weaknesses, liking ourselves even though we have made a mistake or said something we feel sorry we said—we tear ourselves down, belittle ourselves, tell ourselves things which cause us to feel bad, depressed, worried, tense, insecure—in short, we damage ourselves through negative autosuggestion. On the other hand, positive autosuggestion can quiet your quivering nerves, calm you down, alleviate tension and worry, and enable you to cope with almost anything in life. We are always holding mental discussions with ourselves. Whether the discussion is constructive or destructive depends on our attitudes, the kinds of suggestions we give ourselves, and our general philosophy toward life.

Too many people are emotionally crippled by inferiority feelings. These feelings prevent you from doing things which in most cases you are capable of doing. Instead of saying to yourself:

- "I am thoroughly disgusted with myself."
- "I don't think I can do that."
- "My memory is failing—I'm getting old."
- "I have two left feet—I'll never learn to dance."

Say to yourself:

- "I can do anything I set my mind to."
- "I can learn anything I have to—my memory is getting better."
- "If he can do it, I can do it. I'm just as smart."
- "I have confidence in myself."

Imagination plays a very important part in our lives. We act in accordance with our beliefs about ourselves and the suggestions we have given ourselves. If you can picture yourself *succeeding,* you have a good chance of achieving your goal. If you cannot imagine yourself doing something or achieving something, it is unlikely that you will attain it.

I have known several persons who never realized their possibilities until they reached their mid-fifties. Then by reading an inspiring, stimulating book, or listening to a lecture, or talking with a good friend who encouraged them, they were suddenly aroused, as if from a long sleep. Their feelings of inferiority disappeared when they changed their picture of themselves, and they went on to greater and better things in life. Success is relative—it is getting your heart's desire, no matter what it is, and success is welcome at any age.

Jack, a tall, good-looking man of sixty-eight, became a widower two years ago. When he started dating again, he was rather nervous. Would he do the right thing? Say the right thing? He discovered that quite a few women wanted to go dancing. Since he and his late wife had never bothered about learning to dance, he felt lost. One day in class he confessed that he was ashamed to go into the dancing class (offered in adult education for a very nominal fee) because he had "two left feet." "So what?" I said. "Dare to do it! Go into the class. You'll see others there with two left feet, too, but they apparently don't care who knows about it. Besides, after a few lessons you'll find out that you have a left foot and a right foot and you'll learn what to do with them."

He did go into the dancing class—all he needed was a push and a positive attitude. As of this writing, he is living it up. He frequents all the dance spots here in Miami for older people. In fact, he met a lovely widow of sixty-five at one of the dances and seems to have grown younger—he is so full of vitality.

Every day, no matter where I am—in the supermarket, in the drugstore, in the elevator—I hear people making remarks such as: "I'm so nervous, everything upsets me," or "I'm so susceptible to colds, every time I sit in a draft I get a cold," and a thousand other destructive remarks that are detrimental to the nervous system. We have to be careful of the kinds of things we tell ourselves. As you tell yourself you are, so you will become, if you tell it to yourself often enough. *Words have a power that can work either for us or against us.* The nose isn't smart; the nose doesn't know you are sitting in a draft, but your *mind* knows. If you *expect* a cold, you get a cold. Your mind can make you ill and your mind can make you well. It is just as easy to use words that bring calmness, health, and happiness as it is to use words that bring ill health, unhappiness, and nervousness. If you keep telling yourself that you are nervous, you will make yourself more nervous. It is impossible to think one way and feel another way.

HOW TO USE THE BATHROOM TO GET RID OF ANGER CONSTRUCTIVELY

If you derive pleasure from retaliation, it is irrational pleasure. While it is as normal to feel anger as it is to feel love, for health's sake anger *must* be controlled or expressed in a constructive way. For example: You are having a discussion with someone. You don't agree with certain statements. You try to reason with the other person or express your opinions and you are not given the freedom to do so. You may say, "I am getting upset, I can't seem to reach you." (Although there's no law that says you must get upset or angry when you are frustrated.) You are angry and you say, "I would like to get a word in." The other person says, "I do not wish to discuss it anymore." You are left boiling. What do you do? You could hit your head against the wall, but that hurts physically; you could brood about it, which would not only hurt your body chemistry but would also cause you emotional pain. You could break things, you could yell, scream, or retaliate. All are irrational methods of dealing with anger. If you are not given the emotional freedom to express your feelings in a calm and constructive manner, go into the bathroom, let the water run in the tub, shower, or basin, or flush the toilet, and talk to the mirror. Say anything you want—don't censor. Swear, curse, get rid of your anger in the bathroom. "That so and so, right now I hate him. I'd love to smack him," etc. It's far more prudent to talk to the mirror. There's no way to say to a grown-up son or daughter, or even your spouse, "Stand still, I would like to smack your face because you are so frustrating," without creating more friction. Basically you may love the person very much, but when you are frustrated or angry you do not feel lovingly toward the person. And there's no rational reason to feel guilty about it either. When you come out of the bathroom—if you use this technique properly— you will feel "refreshed." Some of my students tell me that they are spending a lot of time in the bathroom lately and as a result there's no friction in their interpersonal relationships.

Other students report to me that they feel silly talking to the mirror. Okay, then don't. Write out your anger. Write everything you would like to say to the person, read it over and over again, and then destroy it. Or if you play golf, every time you hit the ball, pretend mentally you are hitting the person. Or punch a pillow in your home. I remember once when my son was four years old, an older and taller boy hit him while they were playing outdoors and since he couldn't defend himself, he came to me crying. After talking to him for a while, I gave him a pillow to punch and pretend it was the boy who hit him. From that time on he would beat up all the pillows in the house when he was angry or couldn't defend himself (until he learned to take care of himself). I was glad to read after twenty-odd years of advocating the pillow technique that many psychiatrists are suggesting it today. It is far more desirable to use the above methods to get rid of anger than to say to someone you love in a fit of anger: "Drop dead—I hate you." These words fly right into the person's unconscious and remain there. You may have told the person ten thousand times after that, "I love you," and the person may still say, at some future time, "You told me to drop dead."

Of course, there is a still better solution: Don't get angry in the first place. Reason it out; nip it in the bud; say to yourself, "I refuse to respond with anger." Intense anger is most harmful. It can cause a stroke, a heart attack, or lack of sleep. It's really dangerous for a person of advanced years to get too angry. If you permit someone to anger you to the point where you damage yourself, you are permitting that person to hold your life in his hands.

A FOUR-LETTER WORD THAT CAN CHANGE YOUR LIFE

You have something within you that is greater than any obstacle, circumstance, or difficulty you will ever encounter. I call this special quality *grit*. We all, old and young, have it. There is nothing in your life that you cannot modify, change, improve, or adjust when you learn to use your grit.

All of us have courage within us, if we use it. If we don't use it, we haven't got it. It's as simple as that. Ask yourself what it is that you are afraid of. Do you have a "suppose" pattern of thinking and speaking?

- "Suppose I'm rejected?"
- "Suppose I fail?"
- "Suppose I don't make a good program chairman?"
- "Suppose I'm not good enough in bed?"

Suppose is based on fear and worry. Translated, suppose is always saying: "If this should happen or that should happen, I may not be able to take it," or "I may be so embarrassed," or "I'll feel so bad." I asked my students in various classes to verbalize their "supposes" so that they would learn to recognize whether their fears were realistic or not. Here are just a few examples:

Esther, age sixty-four: "Suppose my children or grandchildren should get sick and won't phone me and tell me about it because they know I worry about them."

This fear is unrealistic. Why dwell on illness in the first place? But let's assume her children or grandchildren do get sick and she *is* told about it. What could Esther do now that she knows? She is in Florida and they live in Detroit. Should she fly to Detroit? Because they have a cold? No, Esther is not about to fly to Detroit. Besides, her children would think it ridiculous. But Esther is a very efficient worrier and has nothing else to occupy her time. She did learn, however, that all her worrying and sleepless nights did not cure her grandchild's cold a few weeks ago.

Irene, age sixty-eight: "Suppose my husband dies before me? He has always kept the money aspect of our marriage a secret. I don't know how much money he has or where he keeps anything. He gives me a weekly allowance and pays all the bills. I'm afraid to approach him—he doesn't like to talk about it."

This *is* a realistic fear and Irene must talk about it. It's too bad she waited all these years. She could begin by saying, "Darling, I know you don't like this subject, but we *must* talk about it. I would like you to live to be a hundred, but if anything should happen to you, I won't know what to do. I don't even know if you have a safe-deposit box." Irene should persist whether he likes it or not until the finances are brought out into the open.

Rita, age sixty and very attractive: "Suppose my husband

who is seventy-three decides to leave me for a younger woman? When we go to a club for dinner, I notice how he 'eyes' the women in their thirties dancing with older men in their late sixties and seventies."

This is an unrealistic fear based on an insecurity which stems from her childhood. Her father left her mother when she was a little girl and she has been living with this fear for the forty years of her marriage. Even though she looks much younger than sixty and is rather extroverted, she panics when her husband looks at another woman. She told me during a five-minute break in class that she makes sure he gets enough sex at home so that he won't be "hungry" in case he takes a walk without her for an hour.

Rita soon realized that she had been torturing herself unnecessarily for forty years because of her mother's experience. Also, a woman like Rita needs continuous reassurance from her husband that he loves her. She needs constant demonstrations of his commitment to her.

The "supposes" are endless. Suppose I'm robbed? Suppose my eighteen-year-old granddaughter becomes pregnant? Suppose . . . ?

We need to *use* our grit to face whatever difficulties we may run into. You wouldn't be fearful if you truly *felt* that you could cope with anything, if you believed that you have the courage inside you to see you through anything that might happen. Whatever it is that you're afraid of, grit will pull you through. With this sense of power, you can cope with anything.

We must have perseverance and above all confidence in ourselves. We must look life in the face and *believe* that we can rise above hurt, jealousy, fear, despair, loneliness, and sadness—the power to do so is within every one of us. When we stop holding ourselves back, we automatically go forward.

Tell yourself over and over again, "I have *grit!* I'm not

afraid of anything." Your children and grandchildren may know a few other four-letter words, but *this* four-letter word has *power*.

ATTITUDE IS EVERYTHING

No other word has more impact on your health, youthfulness, happiness, and longevity than the word *attitude*. The way you look at things, what you see in life, your *thoughts* about yourself, others, and the world, your *beliefs*, your personal philosophy of life, all reflect your *attitude*. Your attitude is always showing in whatever you do. It doesn't even have to be verbalized. It is conveyed in your manner, your gait, your posture, your facial expression, the way you sit.

If you focus your attention on all the unpleasant things in your life, that is your attitude. On the other hand, if you focus your attention on the good things in your life, that, too, is your attitude. Push aside the negative factors in your life and concentrate on the positive things. You will feel better, look better, and enjoy life more.

A few months ago, I gave a talk at a men's club on "Attitudes and Optimistic Thinking." I indicated in my talk that optimistic thoughts invigorate and revitalize us. During the question-and-answer period, a man of sixty posed a question. He looked at least ten years older; he was devoid of any vitality. "You talk about optimism, Dr. Rose," he said, "as if it were something new. What's the big deal? There's nothing new about optimism." "You're absolutely correct," I said. "There's nothing new about optimism, but it becomes new for the person who has tried this kind of thinking for the first time and discovers that it works *wonders!* Certainly, there's nothing new about optimism. It's just an attitude. But what an attitude!"

The other day I received a call—the voice on the other end was bursting with life and enthusiasm. "Dr. Rose, it's me." "Who's me?" I asked. "The man who argued with you about optimism—remember? Well, I tried it. It took several weeks for me to realize that my problems are not as bad as I believed them to be. Thinking optimistically *does* work. I feel wonderful! I can't wait until I get up in the morning and get going. I'm planning my life like I'm going to live another fifty years." It was emotionally very rewarding to me, but I must say that *he* deserves the credit, because he accepted this dynamic concept and *used* it. I gave him the lumber, but he built his own house.

Most people are attitudinally handicapped. They find it difficult to believe they can control their reactions to problems and people. When things become tough for you—when everything seems to go against you at one time—how do you react? Do you fall apart? Do you get drunk? Do you rush for a tranquilizer? Do you get sick? Never yield to frustration, despair, or discouragement! You may be knocked down; you're not out. Say to yourself, "I'm going to tackle my problems in a calm and relaxed way. I'll try to solve them as best as I can and if I cannot find an answer to my problem today, I will take an optimistic attitude. "Nothing will defeat me." Lifelong habits of thinking and reacting are hard to break, but it *can* be done. It is a tremendous thing to free yourself from unhealthy attitudes and emotions. Optimistic thinking gives you new hope, new determination, and new self-confidence.

I have a delightful couple in one of my classes. He is eighty-nine, she is eighty-seven. They are *true* optimists. I have never heard a negative remark from them. They sit in the first row, eager to learn. They ask questions and take notes, they are fantastic. When the other students (much younger) ask them how things are, this beautiful couple has one answer: "No day is rotten—it's just that some days are better than others." With that kind of attitude it's no wonder they don't look their ages. I didn't believe it myself until I saw their registration slips. They live a life of optimism, enthusiasm, and joy. They have abundant energy. They never expected to get the illnesses older people are supposed to get. I understand that they have experienced tragedy, have had many problems, but their attitudes have pulled them through and kept them in good health. The optimist gets over his difficulties more rapidly because he believes that life is still good.

We don't have to give up all of our idiosyncracies, hang-ups, or neuroses. We can hold on to some. It makes us more interesting. Let's just give up the neurotic behavior that is making us unhappy, creating illnesses, shortening our lives —let's get rid of *that* kind of behavior. When past mistakes, unpleasant past experiences, or sorrows come into your mind while shaving, making-up, or dressing, you can say to yourself: "Stop it! I no longer want to think about it. The past is over—finished. I will not permit the past to impede my growth."

If you find yourself complaining, "My nerves are shot to pieces," bear in mind that there is nothing the matter with your nerves. The nerves of even a nervous person are perfectly healthy. Nervousness is not an organic disease. It is a functional disorder (meaning psychosomatic). Organic disease implies impairment of the tissues of the organ. When your doctor cannot find anything physically wrong to account for your nervousness, it is assumed that the discomfort is "functional" and due to erratic behavior in the nervous system. It is always a good idea for a nervous person to be examined by a physician. If the doctor finds nothing organically wrong with the person (which will happen in most cases), the trouble lies in the person's personality. Negative emotions do not show up on an X ray.

A neurosis is not based on weak nerves, but on erroneous

ideas. It is not a disease; it is an attitude toward the problems of life. Since a neurosis is curable, we don't have to accept it as a permanent thing. There is help for those who want to change; there is hope for those who want to live life happily.

IT'S NEVER TOO LATE TO CHANGE AND BECOME A NEW YOU

"I'm too old to change" is a destructive attitude and a cop-out. One is *never* too old to change. Another common expression is, "You can't teach an old dog new tricks." Well, I'm not teaching dogs, I'm teaching human beings, and every human being is born with the capacity to change and to grow psychologically. "I can change" is the key to growth. Many of my students have told me that they have changed significantly in terms of their attitudes, emotional responses, and general behavior. I believe them. They look happier, they act happier, and they *are* happier. In fact, some have grown younger-looking before my eyes. If you want to have a ball in life, look younger than your chronological years, ward off illnesses, be more successful, have lots of vitality and vigor, feel good and look good, the first place to start is with your thinking habits. (In later chapters, I'll talk about changing *other* habits that hold you back from achieving optimum health and getting the most out of life.)

It is easier to make over an unhealthy way of thinking than to make over a damaged heart; it is easier to straighten out a warped idea than to straighten out a bent back. Habits of thinking are learned. We have been reinforcing our old habits of thinking and behaving for so many years that they have become automatic. We respond to a given situation with worry, apprehension, anger, or anxiety because we are in the *habit* of doing so. We're not stuck with these destructive patterns—habits can be changed. We *can* achieve emotional well-being. I know that it *is* possible. I know it because I did it and so have thousands of my students over the years.

No one is born with positive or negative attitudes. We usually learn them in childhood and carry them along into adulthood. Betty, a lovely woman of sixty-one, had recently remarried. Her husband, who is sixty-seven, goes into a tantrum whenever she doesn't do what *he* wants her to do. He breaks things in the apartment, kicks the furniture, and sulks. He did the same thing as a child, she told me. Her sister-in-law told her to expect it. I asked her if she wanted to cure him of his tantrums. "I sure do," she said, "but I don't know how. In fact, if he didn't have some wonderful qualities I would have left him shortly after our marriage. It didn't show up until we were married three months."

"It's very simple," I said. "First, ignore the tantrum and go about your business. When he has calmed down, point out to him that you are not his mother and that you do not intend to take such behavior. Tell him that he will have to pay another price for his tantrum, other than the fact that he is damaging his body chemistry and could get a stroke from such anger. *It's going to cost him money.* Tell him you are going to replace everything he breaks or damages *every time* he engages in a tantrum." "Oh, but that could be very costly," she said. "So what? What he is doing to himself could prove to be *more* costly in the long run." Betty did try it. She replaced a few things and charged them. Fortunately for him, when he realized that she meant what she said, his tantrums grew less and less frequent. She taught him that a tantrum doesn't pay off and that communication—clearing the air and talking things over—pays off better.

Do be patient, however. You can't change yourself or your life overnight. As I stated before, you have had your old habits for many years, so don't expect to get rid of destructive responses right away. But you can start right *now* and day by day conquer the behavior that may be keeping you disturbed, ill, depressed, or unhappy. *Live one day at a time.* Practice daily new habits, new responses, new reactions as you go about your business of living. If someone steps on your toes accidentally in the supermarket practice the new habit of not reacting with hostility. After all, the person didn't intentionally step on your foot. He was careless, but why give yourself emotional pain, too? It's enough that you have physical pain. Will it help to ease the pain in your toe if you work yourself up? By practicing the new habit you will be working yourself down. You will be saying to yourself, "Easy does it. He didn't mean to do it. Stay calm." This is just an example of how we can recondition ourselves so that new habits eventually become automatic responses. You must practice every day just as a musician practices or a boxer trains daily.

For example, if you wanted to learn to play the piano, and the teacher gave you a sheet of music to practice all week, you would have to practice to be able to play the piece. If she kept giving you homework and you disregarded it, you would never learn to play the piano. And so it is with changing one's thinking habits. We must *practice* a new way of thinking, a new way of responding to people and situations over and over again until it becomes automatic. By responding unemotionally or with very little emotion to the slightest frustration you will be surprised how well you will handle a greater frustration. You will be reconditioned.

The law of life is: Nothing comes of nothing; we cannot get something for nothing. There is a price to pay for anything that is worthwhile. Life is like a candy machine—you put in your coin and you get your piece of candy. If you don't risk your coin, you get nothing. It will not help us one bit to call the machine bad names, or to be jealous of those who have risked their coins and are enjoying their candy. If we risk our time and effort to change that which can be changed, and the attitudes that make for unhappy living, the chances are very much in favor of our getting what we want out of life. Rational thinking, constructive thinking, positive thinking—it doesn't matter what you call it, it all adds up to a miraculous power. With this incredible power you can deal with whatever happens. You can cope—nothing will overwhelm you. You will experience the ecstasy of being fully alive. What a way to live! You won't be afraid to take emotional risks: rejection, embarrassment, shame, frustration—who cares? "I'm alive and nothing can lick me."

You will be creating a new you. This new you will be reflected in your face and body, in your whole personality. Your face and posture will show less deterioration. You will sit taller, walk taller, by golly, you *are* taller.

How to Have More Energy and Vitality

2

It is not my intention to become too technical or psychoanalytical in this book. However, an understanding of the unconscious forces is invaluable in terms of health, vitality, happiness, success, and longevity. This knowledge can be very helpful to all human beings; therefore, we might as well become acquainted with our own unconscious forces since we are all products of conditioning. When we direct our unconscious properly, it can almost perform miracles.

All of us can learn, to some extent, to master our unconscious, and thereby have less tension and anxiety and get much more out of life.

In defining the unconscious,* it is first necessary to state that we have only *one* mind, but it has two phases: the conscious and the unconscious. The unconscious does not reason, it is not logical, it is very easily impressed. One of the most important points about the unconscious is its openness to suggestion. It believes what it is told. The language of the unconscious is suggestion. This is why it is so impor-

---

*In psychology, the unconscious does not mean *unconsciousness,* as when a person is in a coma, or under an anesthetic, or has an accident and is knocked unconscious. Some writers prefer to use the word *subconscious* as synonymous with unconscious. The psychoanalytic school uses the word *unconscious.* Having been trained psychoanalytically, I prefer to use unconscious.

tant to give ourselves only helpful, healthful, constructive suggestions. The only thing that can make your unconscious work against you is the wrong kind of suggestion. Never tell yourself that you are disgusted, discouraged, miserable, that you fear getting sick, that something dreadful is going to happen, or rejection is too painful to bear, etc. The conscious talks to the unconscious and the unconscious reacts. You can work yourself up and create a lot of tension and anxiety in yourself or you can calm yourself down with your conscious mind. The conscious mind reasons, it is logical, it has awareness; it is the rational part of one's mind.

The unconscious is controlled by suggestion from the conscious. It is invaluable to understand the interaction of the unconscious and conscious. Never tell yourself something is going to happen that you do not wish to happen. For example: "I'm afraid I'll get seasick if I go on that cruise." (If you expect to be seasick, it is likely that you will be seasick.) "I'm afraid I'll fail if I undertake that project." (If you expect to fail, it is likely that you will fail.) "I'm afraid I'll make a fool of myself if I make that speech at the club." There's no end to the "I'm afraid."

Picture yourself doing the very thing you fear and say to yourself: "I can go on that cruise. I'll be fine." "I can undertake that project. I can do anything I set my mind to. I will be successful." "I can make a speech—I have confidence in myself. I have something of value to say and I shall say it effectively."

When you give yourself constructive instructions, your unconscious acts accordingly. You will experience less panic and less apprehension, if any at all.

All of us are brainwashed to some extent, either by certain suggestions we accept from others, or suggestions we have given ourselves. Throughout the years we have developed certain habits—good or bad. These habits are now conditioned reflexes. That is, we respond automatically to situations or people with either fear, anger, worry, irritation, and pessimism, or with love, optimism, and generally constructive ways of thinking and behaving. In other words, our habits are so deeply embedded in us that they are now unconscious actions.

Since most of our behavior and many of our emotions come from the unconscious, we must remember that we can make our unconscious work for us or against us by the kinds of suggestions we give it. It has tremendous power to be used constructively or destructively.

On occasion, the unconscious attempts to trick us and deceive us. It is only interested in the immediate pleasure principle or hedonism. It says, in effect, "I want what I want because I want it, and to hell with the consequences." It doesn't reason—it just wants. However, when we use our unconscious mind properly it can be our most helpful ally. Some people are involved in an internal struggle because the conscious may want one thing and the unconscious another thing. Unless there is harmony between the unconscious and conscious, the person has an internal war going on, which produces tension and anxiety.

We take our thoughts, feelings, and actions for granted, without stopping to wonder where they came from. It isn't what we say consciously, but what is in the unconscious that motivates our behavior. Many of our thoughts, ideas, and attitudes have their origins in the unconscious.

Why do some people lose their heads while others remain calm in the same situation? Anyone who *overreacts* to a little thing that was said or done has something bothering him in the unconscious, and this little thing acted as a stimulus and triggered off the inappropriate reaction. It is no more necessary to have a "temper" or a "nervous" personality than it is to have smallpox. When any kind of behavior has been repeated a sufficient number of times to have become habitual, it becomes a conditioned reflex—an unconscious action.

The unconscious is a vast storehouse. Everything you

have ever learned; all the things that were inculcated in you by your parents, teachers, and peers; traumas and frightening experiences—everything that ever happened to us is in that storehouse. We may have forgotten it consciously, but the unconscious has it all recorded.

Emotions such as hate, jealousy, anger, resentment, are many times pushed into the unconscious (repressed) because the conscious mind dislikes the feelings and may not be able to handle the negative emotions. These emotions may be too painful to be endured consciously, and so we bury the distasteful and/or unacceptable thoughts in the unconscious. Freud called this repressing force the "psychic censor."

Repression is a bad habit like any other bad habit and we can train ourselves not to repress but to express. If you are feeling tense or anxious, ask yourself, "What emotion am I trying to avoid feeling?" There's a reason for your tenseness —you don't just become tense from the air. You are tense because you are attempting to avoid feeling fear, frustration, rejection, or any other negative emotion. Many times we are not aware that we are repressing. It happens automatically if we are in the *habit* of repressing.

It takes an enormous amount of energy to keep undesirable thoughts or emotions repressed. That's why many people are tired all the time. Their energy is being drained. The repressed emotion (or conflict) may manifest itself in fatigue or anxiety or a bad headache or any other physical symptom. In other words, the illness is self-induced. Psychologically, these people would rather have the illness produced by this repression than to have to endure the emotional pain which they experience as the greater agony.

If negative emotions are repressed and not faced or dealt with, they will keep disturbing you in different ways. You may feel upset, depressed, or not feel well physically. Once you become aware of the nonsense you have pushed into the unconscious and face it with courage and permit yourself to feel it and think about it, you become the master of your thoughts and emotions. You will no longer be afraid to face your negative feelings; you no longer need to repress them. In the words of a popular song written some years ago: "It only hurts for a little while."

If you feel tense or anxious or emotionally uncomfortable in some way and you can't see a reason for it consciously, then you must look to the unconscious for the reason. A repressed feeling may be attempting to come out. Let it come out. Tell yourself, "I'm not afraid to think about anything—good or bad." *To break the habit of repression you must think through the unpleasantness and then conquer it.* Tell yourself it's not so terrible to be rejected or frustrated. You may not like it (who does?) but you certainly can still enjoy your life.

How you feel depends on how you tell yourself you will feel. No one can get inside your head and make you feel sick, fearful, or angry. You are the boss of your own mind. You can choose to feel good or bad. When you think through a situation and evaluate it rationally, then back it up with constructive behavior, you are *free*. Tensions and anxieties disappear, psychosomatic ailments disappear—you will feel like a new person.

There are some people who may say: "I don't want to know anything about the unconscious. What I don't know can't hurt me." Psychologically speaking, what you don't know *can* hurt you. When we talk to our unconscious properly using repetitive constructive suggestions, it is manifested in our strength to withstand the pressure of external events and in our ability to tolerate uncertainty without becoming angry or anxious or depressed. If we allow the unconscious to rule us, it can pull us this way and that until we, who should be the masters, become helpless slaves.

Many people do not realize that physical ailments can be produced by negative thoughts. They complain about not feeling well, never realizing that it is of their own making.

It is difficult for some people to see how an intangible thing like a thought can produce a headache or a pain elsewhere in the body. The emotions influence your physical well-being. The key is in your mind, which only you can control.

When an individual can no longer deal with his problem mentally, when he is overwhelmed by it, he converts the problem into a physical illness. This is what is known as a "psychosomatic illness." It isn't as if the person sits down and says to himself, "Now, let's see, what kind of an illness can I give myself to avoid facing my problem?" It doesn't work that way. The person's unconscious steps in, saves him from severe mental anguish, and gives him the illness he is most susceptible to. Some people may develop migraine headaches, others will get colitis or all kinds of aches and pains, and so on. The person is now so busy thinking about his physical ailment and going to doctors for relief of his psychosomatic illness that he never does anything about his real problem. This kind of neurosis is a game that we play with ourselves. The primitive part of the unconscious has an intense craving for an audience. And a psychosomatic illness always gets an audience. Secretly and unconsciously, the person derives certain pleasure in being the object of the solicitous care of his family and friends. The illness also provides an escape from disagreeable duties.

No nervous symptom is what it seems to be. It is a pretender. It pretends to be a physical disease, when primarily it has nothing to do with the body. That is not to say that the pain is not real—certainly if one has a headache or pain, it hurts. What I am saying is that the pain has an emotional origin, which would not manifest itself in the body if the person were able to handle his problem. The body is protesting the frustration or rejection or whatever the person is unable to face. And the person most deluded is the one who has the symptom. Its purpose is to furnish relief to a distracted soul which dares not face itself.

That the unconscious mind has no part in the subterfuge is shown by the fact that when a person understands that he is fooling himself and says to himself, in effect, "There must be a better way of adjusting to my problem and I'm going to find it," his symptoms disappear. An honest desire to get well is a step toward cure.

Sometimes we cannot find an immediate solution to our problem—we may have to wait it out. The ability to withstand the frustration of "waiting it out" calmly is an indication of emotional maturity, of knowing how to utilize the power within us to make our unconscious work for us instead of against us.

The important thing is to *believe* that your unconscious will help you when you call upon it to find solutions for your problems. Without belief or faith, this tireless servant of yours will not work for you. But if you believe in it, it will go to work for you at your slightest command. This power (some people may look upon it as superhuman) has been proven in psychological literature to be the common inheritance of every person.

I have used this tremendous power in my own life. I know it works! When I needed a solution to a problem I thought about it consciously at first, gathered together all the facts regarding my problem, and when I still couldn't find a satisfactory solution, I turned it over to my unconscious. As I relaxed in bed, just before falling asleep, I would give my unconscious the suggestion to find the solution for me or to give me some ideas on how to solve my problem and I would fall asleep with the faith and serenity that my unconscious would deliver. And it did. Sometimes an idea would come to me during the night or in the early morning. Several times a solution would present itself a few days later or a week later. The unconscious cannot be rushed. Once given the suggestion, it goes about its business trying to work it out. Do not reject any ideas that come to you. Evaluate the solution, and if it seems reasonable to your conscious mind, *act on it.* Without action, you are not making use of the power within you.

POINTS TO REMEMBER ABOUT MAKING YOUR UNCONSCIOUS WORK FOR YOU

- The unconscious is amenable to control by suggestion.
- Learn to use the power constructively. Say, "I can and I will." Do not say, "I will try." This suggestion indicates doubt.
- Every time we get angry our vitality shrinks; the amount of shrinkage is in proportion to the violence of the outburst.
- Joyful emotions invigorate. Sorrowful emotions depress. Pleasurable emotions stimulate. Painful emotions burden. Satisfying emotions revitalize. Negative emotions sap one's strength.
- The unconscious can be convinced of *any* attitude if repeated often enough. It's the repetition that produces the results.
- When you are in a positive state of mind you are never nervous or disturbed. In fact, the more positive you are, the better your control over your entire system.
- The conscious mind feeds information to the unconscious and then forgets it. The unconscious never forgets.
- Your unconscious is your friend as long as

you use it properly. Used improperly it is your enemy.
- Become aware of your habits. Some are useful, helpful, and constructive—others are harmful and useless. Discard the harmful habits and practice new ones. Make the new habits automatic.
- Do not become discouraged when things go wrong. Get on with your life, undisturbed. If you don't weaken when things are not going right for you, you will grow stronger and stronger. You will finally have the strength you need to carry on and reach your goal.
- We speak of "lucky" people—lucky in health, lucky in love—but we do not realize that a large part of their success is due to the superabundant vitality and mental vigor that comes from right thinking. If more people were aware that "as a man thinks in his unconscious" so he is, they would be better off. What we believe controls our actions. If one believes that he will always have a hard time, that he will never achieve his goals, that he is "unlucky," he will be as he believes. But if he believes otherwise—that he, too, has the opportunity to do more, to be more, to have more (provided he is willing to work for it), he will probably see a change in his life in a short time.

STOP FEELING GUILTY

When you feel guilty you are cheating yourself of happiness and serenity. You push away, consciously or unconsciously, the very things you need to feel alive and experience a sense of well-being. And in nonverbal language you may even be saying, "Look at me, world—see how I suffer—don't you feel sorry for me?"

Several months ago I was giving a lecture on "Guilt Feelings and the Older Person" to one of my classes. I asked my students how many would like an "acquittal"—freedom from guilt and freedom from self-punishment. Almost every hand in the class went up. What did they feel guilty about? What monstrous crimes had they committed? Dear, gentle Ruth who never raised her voice to anyone, always polite and smiling. Jack, quiet and reserved, who didn't even have the heart to kill the water bug that crawled under his feet. But Ruth had an ulcer and some other stress-related ailments, and Jack had high blood pressure and other ailments with an emotional origin. These nice, quiet, beautiful people had never learned how to shake off guilt.

I asked them to voice some of their guilt feelings. Here are some of the "crimes" they felt guilty about:

- "I spanked my son when he was nine years old. I can't forget it. Every time I look at him I feel guilty. He's thirty-nine now."
- "My grandchildren live in Chicago. When I hear that they have a cold during the winter months, I get sick. I feel guilty because I live in a beautiful climate."
- "Perhaps I should have done more for my deceased wife. I don't know what—but it bothers me."
- "I'm having such a good time with the money

my deceased husband left me. I feel guilty."
- "I made so many mistakes—I could have been a rich man today, if only I had listened to my wife."
- "I hate myself. When I visit with my son and daughter-in-law I should put a zipper on my mouth. I say things I shouldn't say and feel rotten after I leave them."
- "I'm having a romance with a widower. He's alone, I'm alone—why should I feel guilty? I don't mind admitting it in class, but I wouldn't like my grown children to know about it."
- "The 'dirty old man' image haunts me, but I still think about sex and engage in it whenever possible."
- "My friends make me feel bad because I'm dating a woman twenty-five years younger than I. I'm sixty."
- "Every time I'm frustrated I eat like there's no tomorrow. I feel guilty afterward because my doctor *ordered* me to lose thirty pounds."
- "I have a first cousin who is so bizarre-looking that I am ashamed to have her visit me. When she calls I have an excuse for not having her over. I wouldn't want the neighbors to know that she is part of my family. I hate myself sometimes for trying to hide her. She really is a good person."

That's just a partial list of the "crimes." Can you identify with any of them?

Guilt Can Make You Ill

Shame and embarrassment are cousins of guilt. When you feel guilty you don't like yourself. You're in pain when you hate yourself. You scream silently rather than risk being unlikable. As a result, many mild, gentle, reserved people develop high blood pressure, heart disease, and many other illnesses. Needless to say, you cannot enjoy life when you feel guilty.

You Deserve an Acquittal

Whatever your particular guilt is, acquit yourself. If there is something you can do to rectify things, do it—if not, forget it and forgive yourself. You don't have to punish yourself. You have served your sentence over and over again. You have had enough mental anguish.

We all make mistakes, we all blunder. So what? None of us is perfect. Isn't it foolish to give yourself a life sentence because you made some mistakes, or you were having fun when in the court of your own mind you felt you should have been cleaning out closets or the garage or cooking a ten-course dinner?

How long should you go on whipping yourself emotionally because you spanked your child thirty years ago?

If you are having an affair and not hurting anyone, either find a way to keep doing what you're doing without feeling guilty, or quit what you're doing. You have a choice.

You have to convince yourself that feeling guilty is useless—it doesn't help you or change the situation. Give yourself a mental shampoo—wash out the guilty feelings and start living it up. Whenever you're in doubt as to whether you should feel guilty or not, ask yourself, "Am I hurting anyone by this action?" If not, have a ball.

Past fifty we can't afford to harbor guilt, hate, anger, resentment, or jealousy. It will eat us up. We have to take care of our bodies. The mind talks to the body and the body talks back—in illness or in good health.

How to Conquer Guilt

Miriam, a widow of sixty, was sent to me by her medical doctor. She had lost her husband two years ago and was slowly sinking. She blamed herself for not taking better care of him. He died suddenly of a heart attack that had nothing to do with her at all. Her doctor could do nothing more for her except deaden her emotional pain with drugs, which he refused to do any longer.

"I don't know what to do with myself," she said. "Life is meaningless, empty—I'm so alone."

Heavy beads of perspiration fell from her face. Tears filled her eyes. Misery was stamped on her face. She spoke in rasping tones. She held my arm as she talked and I got the feeling that she was holding on to keep from sinking. Since her husband's death she had taken no interest in social activities or hobbies. Friends and acquaintances no longer enjoyed being with her, which made her feel more worthless. She watched television alone every evening. Now all she felt was emotional pain and loneliness. She did not know what she wanted.

"How do I begin to live again?" she asked. She seemed to be at the very end of her resources. I felt compelled to help her find a beginning—a belief in the possibility of a new life.

I explained to her that nursing grief month after month, or year after year, is a crime against oneself, and against all others with whom one comes in contact. It does absolutely no good to anybody, especially the grieving person. Such mourning is only *self-pity*. I also told her that although the pleasure and comfort from her husband may have gone out of her life, she still has joyous memories of what was once enjoyed. Rather than continue to make herself and others miserable, she had to make an attempt to begin a new life.

I further explained that the only thing that could save her was a change in attitude and *action*. I suggested as the first step that she come into my class. She would meet and mingle with others who had gone through the same thing. She would gather more knowledge in terms of how to survive and her therapy would be cut in half.

She had indicated in our counseling sessions that she used to paint, a long time ago. I insisted she paint something—anything—and bring it to class. She did, and received many compliments regarding her painting. In fact, one student wanted to buy it. She became motivated and kept on painting.

Somehow fresh strength flowed into her, encouraging her and enabling her to continue painting and seeking other activities. She discovered she had the power within herself to find a new meaning in life. She began to speak more calmly. "By some strange miracle, I am beginning to live again," she said.

A transformation had taken place. She looked youthful, her face was alive, her smile was radiant. She stopped blaming herself and chose to change her life.

Had Miriam continued to blame herself for her husband's death, her guilt feelings would have destroyed her. Also, had she not put out the effort to gain some recognition—from her paintings and other activities—and raise her self-esteem, she would have continued to go downhill.

Arthur, a tall, well-built man of sixty-six, lost his wife four months ago. He was very depressed and lonely—the nights especially were very bad, he told me. He was a former student of mine. I remembered his vigorous movements and his smiling, unlined face. When he came to see me, he was quite changed: his shoulders drooped, he looked haggard. He, too, was suffering from guilt feelings. Not because of his wife—he had done all that was humanly possible for her. He had been a good husband; he adored her and showed it.

(They were both in my class.) He felt guilty because the neighbors were giving him "dirty looks" because he was dating a lady who lived in the same building he lived in. He told me in our counseling session that when he met this lady and found that he liked her and could go to the theater, dinner, and movies with her, he began to feel better. He had found a companion and was coming out of his depression. And then the neighbors went to work on him. He heard remarks such as: "She's not cold in her grave yet and he's running around already—what a bastard."

He couldn't handle it. He stopped seeing the lady and went into a depression again. That's when he came to see me. He wanted to know if what he was doing was wrong. Should he continue to see the lady (who was indeed very understanding) or should he suffer? Should he please his neighbors or himself? Not only his neighbors felt this way, but also a few of his so-called friends thought it was *terrible* to date so soon.

Who is to say how long one should grieve? Some grieve for one month, realize that life must go on, and reconnect with the world. They don't love their deceased spouse any less—it's just that they have the ability to bounce back quicker than others. Then there are others who need a longer period to mourn.

Arthur didn't even know how to boil an egg. He was lost. You don't need much intelligence to boil an egg, but there are some men who throughout their married life never see what the kitchen looks like. Arthur happens to be intelligent, but when the emotions step in, reason steps right out. He couldn't think rationally. I asked him what his neighbors did for him. Did he get solace, comfort, perhaps a dinner from them? Breakfast? Chicken soup? *Nothing.* Should he permit them to manipulate him and instill guilt in him? No!

Whatever he could do for himself to survive physically and psychologically is *right.* And if this new lady friend helped him to survive, then it is morally, spiritually, and psychologically good.

He made the final decision as to what to do with his life. He phoned to tell me, a few weeks later, that he had moved out of the building and had resumed his relationship with the lady. He became his own judge and acquitted himself.

Depression, morose thoughts, and guilt feelings must be banished, for these devils not only disturb the mind, but also injure the body by developing poisonous cells.

HOW TO USE IMAGERY TO ACHIEVE WHAT YOU WANT

Men often become what they believe themselves to be. If I believe I cannot do something, it makes me incapable of doing it. But when I believe I can, then I acquire the ability to do it even if I didn't have it at the beginning.

Mahatma Gandhi

Self-depreciation is a crime against yourself. If you believe that you are a weakling, a failure, a coward, ugly, or lazy, not only will you act like that, but most people will also treat you as such. People respond to the value one places on oneself. If you wish to change your conception of yourself, visual imagery will help you achieve what you want. Forming visual images of yourself as you would like to be influences the unconscious. Imagery is a powerful force. It is not some kind of hocus-pocus. It is a very effective psychological concept. Visualize your goal—whatever you want to achieve. When you picture it in your mind you are planting an idea in your unconscious and your unconscious will strive for realization of your goal. Do you want to lose weight? How much? Ten pounds? Twenty pounds? See yourself in your mind twenty pounds lighter—nice and trim. Find an old photo of yourself when you were slimmer (if you haven't got one, use someone else's slim body with the same proportions), cut off the face, and paste on a picture of your face as it is now. Keep looking at the photo. Impress it on your unconscious. Mentally see yourself getting slimmer and slimmer. Walk around saying to yourself: "I want to lose weight. I love being slender. I no longer care for junk food or high-calorie foods. I no longer care for ice cream, candy or cake." When you look at any kind of food that is bad for you in terms of your weight or health, visualize the word *poison* in your mind. Let it flash across your mind several times. If you see the junk food in your mind as delicious and delectable, you will not be able to abstain from it without feeling frustrated and irritable. But if you look upon it as *poison,* you eventually will not be able to eat it. The unconscious only wants what is pleasurable. It rejects that which is not pleasurable. So if you convince your unconscious that ice cream or any other food you shouldn't eat is poison, you will not feel frustrated—you won't want it.

I must say that no diet can work for you for long if you try to use will power instead of your imagination to abstain from certain foods. This is why so many people "cheat" and cannot stay on a diet: "I'll just eat it today—tomorrow I'll diet." They use their power of imagery destructively instead of constructively. They look at the food and say, "Oh boy, that looks delicious, but I have will power, I'm not going to eat it"—and then all day they are frustrated or miserable. It's not will power that does the trick—it's imagination. If you say to yourself, "That pie is poison. It looks horrible. I don't know how anyone can eat it," it is very likely that eventually you will lose your desire for the food that has been putting weight on you and you will *not* be frustrated. Eating properly will become a habit.

Constructive visual imagery means using your imagination to picture only what is good, what is beneficial, and what you wish to realize. If you are a worrier you are using imagery destructively. You are visualizing in your mind negative results or disastrous results and that's why you worry. *Change the picture!* Do not see yourself mentally having a hard time. Do not imagine yourself in adverse circumstances. See yourself in your mind finding better and better circumstances. See yourself gaining the best out of life. Associate your future with the best that you can think of. Envision yourself becoming more healthful and vigorous in body. The imagination has a tremendous power to promote health, abundant energy, and vitality. Through visual imagery you will get such full control over your feelings that you can always feel the way you want to feel, no matter what the circumstances may be.

Many people believe that because they have had a "temper" all their lives they can't change at age fifty, sixty, or beyond. They usually say, "I can't help it—that's the way I am." When a student or client of mine tells me this, I invariably say, "Tell me, whose unconscious is it? Yours or someone else's? *You* are still responsible for your temper, which is now so embedded in your unconscious that you respond automatically. You can control your temper through visual imagery. You have a picture in your mind as a person with a temper—one who screams, rants, and raves over the slightest frustration or disparaging remark. Change your self-image. See yourself as the kind of person who reacts calmly to frustration, traffic jams, to anything that has previously brought out your temper. Project an image of yourself reacting to circumstances with equanimity."

A successful visual image must be created before you can achieve anything. You can picture yourself in a previous fearful situation reacting without fear. You can imagine yourself relaxed and calm with no tension, no anxiety.

William, a tall, heavy-set man, walked with slumped head and shoulders. His body language indicated burdens, inferiorities, self-depreciation. He told me he had derived great benefit from imagery. He began to picture different results. He envisioned himself handling whatever he had to do with emotional strength and confidence. His feelings of inadequacy were conquered—his tendency toward self-depreciation vanished. He began to walk with an air of great importance. He felt nine feet tall, he said.

Whatever you want to learn—tennis, golf, dancing—first get expert instruction, then practice the *proper* movement in your mind over and over again. See yourself doing it until you feel that it's the very best you can do. The way you practiced it in your imagination will be precisely the way you will do it.

Bess, a very charming woman of fifty-five, told me that she never goes to a big party where she knows only the hostess without first practicing in her imagination how she will greet each person. She envisions herself being introduced to strangers at the party and greeting them with poise and confidence, making conversation and enjoying herself. If you shake with fear every time you have to meet strangers at social functions, use visual imagery to overcome your fear. See yourself in the presence of strange people perfectly composed, talking, laughing, and being completely at ease.

If it is making a speech that throws you into a panic, use the same technique. Project images of yourself that will make you feel good. Go so far as to picture exactly what you will wear. See yourself composed, facing your audience, delivering your speech with ease, and finally visualize the audience applauding you. Do this several times a day until you feel comfortable. You will save yourself a lot of misery.

If you feel angry at someone and you know that you cannot reason with this person because he has a closed mind, take a brisk walk, and in your *imagination* tell the person off—don't censor. The exercise and ventilating—actually seeing the person in your mind and letting him have it—reduces the tension and dissipates the anger.

Use imagery to become a "new you." See yourself looking younger and acting younger. Picture yourself doing the things you want to do with confidence and serenity. You have to give your unconscious the right pictures. Only visualize that which you wish to realize. *Never picture what you don't want to happen.* As you visualize the new you act as if you are already a changed person. You will say and do instinctively what you have envisioned.

IT PAYS TO LAUGH

In laughter, the pain of the heart is eased.

Proverbs 14:13

It is very important for your health and happiness to laugh heartily. Find something to laugh about every day—cartoons, comic strips, humor magazines, a comedy program on television, a funny movie, jokes, etc. A good hearty laugh can benefit your lungs and respiratory system. It may even prevent or lessen illnesses. It certainly reduces your tensions and stress. A human being cannot feel two opposite emotions at the *same* time. While you are laughing you cannot be angry, depressed, or sad. After a hearty laugh it is likely that you will feel better. If you wish, afterward, you can go back to feeling sad. The choice is yours.

You can *teach* yourself to laugh if it doesn't come spontaneously. I really learned to laugh heartily when I was in college working on a second degree. I needed a certain psychology course that was given that semester by a professor who commanded us to laugh as soon as we walked into the classroom and sat down. I mean *commanded!* Anyone who didn't laugh couldn't stay in his class. What was there to laugh about? He didn't tell jokes. We were all scared. We needed his course. Some of us began to chuckle. (My own "laughter" prior to that course was a kind of chuckle.) "I didn't say chuckle," he shouted, "I said laugh." We really thought he was crazy, not knowing his real purpose that first day in class. When a few students really began to laugh, it became contagious. We all looked at each other and laughed. The whole class was belly laughing. Then he screamed, "Stop!" And we had to stop on command. Five minutes of belly laughing and we all felt wonderful—no more tension, just a feeling of well-being. He then told us his purpose: He wanted us to be relaxed so that we could absorb what he was teaching, and laughter eliminates nervous tension and clears the mind. Even though we *forced* ourselves to laugh it still had a beneficial effect on us both mentally and physically. So each week when we came to class we had to laugh for five minutes. The day of the final examination he ordered us to laugh a little longer. Everyone did exceedingly well on the exam. I fooled him—now I can say it. All week I read jokes, and when I came to class, I thought about the jokes and roared.

Philip, sixty-eight, is a picture of health because he has a happy frame of mind. When he says something funny in class, I laugh heartily. I appreciate it. A few of my students, unfortunately, do not. Their attitude is, "I came to learn psychology—I didn't come to listen to jokes." They take life too seriously. They forget that no one gets out of the world alive. However, I have trained many of my students to laugh heartily, even though it was rather difficult for some.

Even if you are beset with problems, you can still laugh at a joke. Laughter helps you to cope with life's problems. If you can't see any humor in a particular joke or humorous situation, it doesn't mean there's something terribly wrong with you. Perhaps you haven't developed attitudes of laughter, joy, and appreciation of humor. Even if a joke is corny, laugh—what have you got to lose? Only your tensions, boredom, and *emotional constipation.*

A person who laughs easily is far more attractive than one with a blank, grouchy face. No matter what triggers the laughter, remember that it's the greatest medicine. You cannot be miserable and laugh at the *same* time.

I might as well give you a laugh (I hope) before you go on to the next section. One of my students told me he called his stockbroker the other day. "Jim, what's the latest dope on Wall Street?" "My son!" replied the stockbroker.

How to Retard Aging

3

Can the aging process really be slowed down? Yes! Is there something you can do about it? You bet your life there is:

Think right
Eat right
Exercise right
Live right

What a team! You can speed up the aging process or slow it down. The more negative stress you have, the more rapidly you will age. Prolonged hostilities, jealousies, apprehension, anxiety, worry, and fear increase tension. These negative emotions cause a person to age prematurely. Developing good emotions—*thinking right*—is the *first* rule in retarding aging. This may be one of the reasons why some people look so much younger than their actual years and others look so much older. To stop stress from mounting, nip it in the bud. Tell yourself, "I've got to get rid of this stressful feeling right now!" Change your thoughts immediately to optimistic, cheerful thoughts and take some positive action.

Barbara, age fifty-two, divorced for five years, is always in a hurry. She has recently developed high blood pressure, looks weary and much older than she is. She is constantly tense. She gets up at the last minute to go to work. If she is caught in traffic, she sits in her car and stews. Her internal motor is racing, too, while she's sitting in the car. She just can't relax. If she would get up a little earlier, she wouldn't make herself so tense. Her internal motor would not be shouting, "Hurry, hurry, hurry." She could also say to herself, "Be calm, relax," a hundred times a day if necessary and follow through with calm and relaxed behavior no matter what came up.

Perhaps you are having a rough day today. Your grandchildren or relatives are visiting with you or staying over. You're tired of constantly catering to them, cooking and serving. Take a break for ten minutes. Go into your bedroom. Close the door and lie down with your feet twelve to fifteen inches higher than your head. Close your eyes and think serene thoughts, calm thoughts, cheerful thoughts. You will be surprised what this will do for you. You will feel a surge of energy flowing into your body. You will feel composed. You will get rid of the stress and tension before it knocks you out. Take a few breaks a day if necessary. If you are a working person, find a spot somewhere (even the bathroom will do) where you can be alone for a few minutes. Sit down and just talk to yourself. "Easy does it—be calm—relax." It sure beats a coffee and cigarette break. The former permits your body to regenerate itself; the latter is harmful to your body.

If you are aging prematurely, then you are doing something to yourself that is aging you. It *is* possible to be revitalized. Cells will not stay young forever, but you *can* retain your youth for a long time. The body has the ability to regenerate itself. Ask yourself: "What am I doing to myself that is inhibiting the regeneration process and my youthfulness?" Here are some of the ways in which you inhibit the regeneration process:

Eating the wrong food
Too much alcohol
Smoking

Not enough exercise
Not enough sleep
Negative thoughts and emotions
Not dealing with your problems correctly
Giving in to stress

If you get rid of the destructive habits that are interfering with the regeneration process, you can become youthful again. I don't mean to imply that once you have aged a great deal, all of it can be erased; but premature aging can be reversed. Don't let another day go by—start now to regain your youthfulness. The longer you wait the harder it will be to restore it.

Underactivity ages people rapidly. I overheard a conversation between two men in the elevator the other day. "Hi, Al. How do you feel?" "Lousy—what can you expect at sixty-five?" I see Al sitting in the lobby when I leave for class. I see Al sitting in the lobby when I come home in the afternoon. And I see Al sitting in the lobby when I leave for my evening class. What *can* you expect from disuse? Al looks much older than sixty-five. He is deteriorating. Underactivity is a form of abuse.

No matter how old you are, vitality can be fostered. This "vital power" is not limited. Outward signs of aging do not mean that you can't be full of zest and vitality, provided you are not in ill health. Clara, a dynamic woman of seventy, has a hang-up regarding her age. On the registration form she put down "middle-aged" on the line where it indicated birthday. The first time she did this, I told her she had to give me her birthday (school board rules) or I could not register her. She whispered her age to me and told me about her hang-up. When this went on for a few semesters (she kept signing up and putting down "middle-aged" so that others would not see her age in the class), I finally said to her one day, "Stop worrying about your age. Inside, where it really counts, you're young—you're full of vigor and vitality." "I know," she said, "but outside, where it shows, I'm old."

A friend of mine also has "age" phobia. "Every time I think about getting old I become depressed—I don't want to get old." "I don't mean to be harsh," I said, "but if you don't want to get old, you will have to kill yourself while you are still middle-aged."

For some people, "senior citizen" has a negative connotation. They perceive themselves now as *old*. In fact, many of my students do not like to be called senior citizens. So I gave them a new title: "You are 'experienced citizens of a new life' as far as I'm concerned," I said. They liked it. Others said, "I like to call myself a 'mature citizen,' even though I may not be so mature, psychologically." Call yourself anything you like—only think *young*. If you are getting something free or half price because you are sixty-five or over, then on *paper* you are a senior citizen. Otherwise, in your mind, believe that you are ageless.

I love this story about Harold. He just turned sixty-five and his friends started kidding him and telling him that now he had better take it easy because he's "old." The negative suggestions finally got to Harold and he began to experience all kinds of aches and pains. He went to his physician for a check-up. "You're okay," the doctor said, "nothing wrong with you. Take a mouthful of brandy after breakfast. It will perk you up." "Oh no, I couldn't do that," Harold said, "my wife would never condone it. She doesn't approve of any kind of liquor. She would throw it out." "Well, then," the doctor replied, "take a colored bottle and fill it up with brandy and keep it in the bathroom. While you are shaving, take a nip." Harold obeyed the doctor's orders. Two weeks later Harold's wife went to the doctor for her annual check-up. "How is your husband?" the doctor asked. "Oh fine," the wife replied, "he has rosy cheeks, he's cheerful, but you know, doctor, I think he's becoming senile." "What makes you say that?" "Well," the wife answered, "he shaves six times a day now."

We have to work at staying youthful and healthy. Here are some tips on how to retard aging for both men and women:

- Never let the words, "I'm getting old," come from your lips.
- Adopt a positive philosophy of life.
- Develop the ability to handle pressure and shake off tension and anxiety.
- If you have retired from your business or profession, don't retire from life. Have a second career the second time around—even if it's volunteer work.
- Eat only that which contributes to the health of your body. Good nutrition is essential in terms of retarding the aging process.
- Get some form of exercise (even if it's just walking). Keep moving. Don't sit all day—it's bad for circulation.
- Get enough sleep. This is an individual thing. Some do well and look well on five hours of sleep a night—others need seven, eight or more.
- Avoid heavy drinking.
- Don't smoke (smokers wrinkle faster than nonsmokers).
- If your lifestyle is aging you prematurely—change it!
- Enjoy your life.

GET RID OF EMOTIONAL CONSTIPATION

Some people in advanced years develop what may be termed "emotional and intellectual constipation." They hold themselves back from enjoying life. Their attitudes have hardened in them like cement. They have become rigid and inflexible. They can't loosen up. It is emotional and intellectual constipation that interferes with the person's ability to handle his problems and adapt to changing circumstances.

This condition can be alleviated just as one can alleviate physical constipation. You wouldn't walk around with physical constipation for years without attempting to do *something* about it. Why walk around with emotional and intellectual constipation? Make a decision to do something about it!

- Examine your attitudes and values today. Are they outdated? Are they helping you to live better? If not, change them.
- Welcome change. Change means growth. Without change there can be no growth.
- Do things differently. Be flexible. If you have been marketing in one supermarket for years, try another, just to teach yourself flexibility. If you walked one route for weeks or months, take a different route. If you drive, deliberately take different routes to reach your destination—just for change.
- Read different kinds of books and newspapers.
- Avoid becoming set in your ways.
- Learn new skills; welcome new ideas.

- Dare to wear bright colors if you have worn conservative clothes all your life.
- Remember that enthusiasm creates energy.
- Dare to live it up! Loosen up!

Any activity that is not routine for us is refreshing to our minds and bodies. To remain vital and flexible we need new activities. Older people are perfectly capable of learning new skills. It may take a little longer, but as long as the desire to learn is there the person will learn. Sarah learned to drive at sixty-seven because her husband was ill and could no longer drive. Dorothy, at seventy-five, learned to speak French fluently because she is planning a trip to Paris.

If the mind is not exercised enough, it becomes stiff. Don't narrow your life—broaden it. Your new life can be exhilarating.

YOU CAN LIVE TO BE ONE HUNDRED

Do you really want to live long? Do you love life? Are there places you haven't seen yet? Things you haven't done yet? Do you want to see your grandchildren (or friends' grandchildren) married? I'm sure all of my readers would answer yes to the above questions. Well, then, don't become your own executioner.

Ruling out accidents, tell yourself that you *are* going to live long, that you *are* going to have lots of zest and vitality, and that you will do everything in your power to *lengthen* your life—not shorten it.

It *is* possible to enjoy good health in advanced years. Do not accept the outdated theory that ill health or disease is inevitable as one gets older. It is not due to the passage of time. It is due to a pessimistic philosophy of life, improper eating habits, negative emotions, and the *expectation* of illness. How can your body chemistry be right if your thinking is not right? There is ample scientific evidence indicating that we can live to be one hundred or more, even if our own parents died at an earlier age, provided we take care of ourselves mentally and physically. This means we have to guard our health and get rid of "killer" habits and attitudes. For example, we don't swallow poison, because we know that it would have an immediate and fatal effect. On the other hand, we do not see *immediate* effects of smoking, so we continue to smoke and rationalize doing so: "Well, I can't give up everything I enjoy." I'm not asking you to give up everything—only those things that interfere with the body's ability to renew and repair itself. The body has built-in means of self-renewal, but you've got to give it a chance to regenerate itself. You can learn to enjoy other things. Instead of telling yourself, "I enjoy smoking," how about telling yourself, "I no longer enjoy smoking—in fact, I hate it. My lips burn every time I put a cigarette between my lips. My throat burns. I can't smoke anymore. I can't stand it!" Remember, the unconscious only wants that which is pleasurable. If you keep telling yourself you enjoy smoking, you won't be able to quit. If you convince your unconscious that you hate it, you will be planting a seed in your unconscious. In a few weeks, if you really are determined to quit smoking, you will not be able to smoke. You will experience the symptoms that you suggested to your unconscious.

At any age, you can clean out your arteries—get rid of cholesterol deposits and revitalize your muscles and joints—if you are willing to work at it. I will elaborate more on nutrition in the next chapter. If you love your body, be concerned with what you put into it.

There are many activities that one can indulge in to prevent premature aging. Many courses are given in adult education (especially for retired persons). Many of my students are also taking courses in ceramics, painting, dancing, sewing, yoga, typing, languages. You name it—adult education is offering it. "That's not my cup of tea," you may be thinking. Okay, so find something else to recharge your energy. By stimulating your brain you automatically stimulate your body, which may actually prolong your life. *Mental and physical activity cultivate the will to live.* Physical inactivity leads to poor circulation. Let's not fear growing older—let's fear inactivity.

Poor posture is another enemy of longevity. The resistance of the lungs is lowered when posture is bad. Whether you sit, walk, or stand, pull in your stomach and straighten your back—don't slouch. Gradually you will strengthen your abdominal muscles and your back muscles and you will have a natural girdle. You will look younger, too.

Here are some additional tips that could help you to live to be one hundred:

- Learn to relax—give yourself positive instructions.
- Have fun. There is medicine in fun, but there's no fun in medicine.
- Lose weight if you are overweight and keep it off.
- Negative stress leads to deterioration of body tissues and organs. Learn how to avoid it.
- Laugh a lot. He who laughs, lasts.
- Exercise (if your physical condition permits) or walk, walk, walk.
- Get sufficient sleep for your body. If you feel better with more sleep, don't listen to anyone who tells you you can get by on less sleep. Be your own doctor when it comes to sleep.
- Take a "stretch" break or "walking" break instead of a coffee break.

- Take up hobbies, pursue new interests.
- Eat less to live more.
- Develop a positive and optimistic approach to life.
- Don't concert your problems and/or frustrations into illnesses—learn how to take it on the chin. Nothing is terrible or horrible unless you think it is.
- Make happiness rather than unhappiness a habit.
- Always bear in mind that the best way to lengthen your life is not to shorten it.

HOW TO STAY YOUTHFUL LONGER

Staying youthful longer does not mean that you will *never* change physically. It does mean that you can *look younger* than you are as you grow older. It also means maintaining the wonderful qualities of enthusiasm, curiosity, and flexibility.

I was on a three-day cruise to the Bahamas two years ago. I was delighted to see so many people in their late sixties and seventies "living it up." They were absolutely radiant —they lit up the ship with their animation. They were dancing, singing, telling jokes, performing—they were alive! One lady of sixty-seven said to me, "These are the best years of my life. My earlier years were joyless ... so much struggle rearing children, etc. I'm free now to do what I want."

Men and women are as old as they make themselves or as young as they allow themselves to be. Never tell yourself that you are too old to do this or that, for your thoughts will be pictured on your face and you will have a prematurely old expression on your face.

Manny is in his late sixties. In many ways he was much

younger than a man of forty until his friends reminded him repeatedly that he was "older" now and should act his age. Manny deposited those pessimistic thoughts in his mental bank account. It didn't take long before he looked older, acted older, and *became* older.

Don't listen to people who say to you, "Act your age." It's a destructive remark. There's no law that says you must act your age, except your own law, if that's what you believe. You may be sixty or seventy or eighty and feel like forty. Act the way you feel and not the way someone else says you *should* feel or *should* act. One good answer to "act your age" is: "I am! I'm acting my psychological age. I feel young." Psychological age is far more important than chronological age.

Michael, age sixty-five, was dating a divorced woman of forty-five who lived in the same condominium. They went to all the social functions held at the condominium. Everyone accepted them and said nothing of the age difference. Bernice, a lovely widow of sixty-one in the same condominium, came to the social functions with a stunning man of forty-nine that she had been dating for some time. She was blooming—she looked younger and felt younger. Many comments were spread, which eventually reached her ears: "She ought to act her age . . ." "She must think she's getting younger . . ." "She ought to be ashamed." Bernice felt uncomfortable and eventually gave up the man although she was extremely fond of him. She couldn't live with the disapproval of her "friends" and neighbors. She felt depressed and lonely. Finally, she came to the realization that her so-called friends were jealous of her. They discouraged her because they couldn't stand to see her blossoming. The man was truly fond of her and had wanted the relationship to develop. I advised her to call him up and find out if he was still available. He was very happy to hear from her and they got together again. She informed him about the "comments" and how uncomfortable they had made her. He reassured her that the age difference had never bothered him. They are still together and the last I heard they were thinking of getting married. She made up her mind that she was going to have a ball in life and if her friends and neighbors didn't approve—too bad!

Romantic feelings do not belong to youth alone. One of my students told me this story: Sally, age sixty-five, went to a senior citizens dance and danced practically all evening with Joseph, who was seventy. When the music stopped at the end of the evening, he asked Sally if she would have some coffee with him in a nearby restaurant. "Oh, come to my apartment," she said, "I make a much better cup of coffee and I also have homemade cake." This appealed to Joseph. "By the way, Sally, suppose I try to make love to you after we have coffee—would you scream for help?" "Why," she asked, "do you *need* help?"

Romance is another name for the joy a man and woman get in living. Romantic feelings do not apply to sexual pleasure only. You can be romantic with someone of the opposite sex by sharing ideas, experiences, by visiting interesting places, and listening to music together. Romance keeps one youthful a long time.

Many people enjoy a massage to keep their muscles elastic and their bodies supple. That's fine. But there is still another way of preserving youthful elasticity, and that is, to *massage the mind* with youthful, beautiful, cheerful thoughts.

Some people grow old prematurely because they don't know how to keep young. Instead of looking backward, let us look forward and put as much variety and as many interests into our lives as possible. Monotony and boredom are great age producers.

In the next chapter, I will discuss how to help yourself biologically through good nutrition and exercise. Right now, what is important is your psychological age. How old do you feel? If you didn't know your age, how old would you say you were? I asked some of my students the same question. Here are their comments:

Vigorous John, age seventy-two: "In no way do I feel like an old man. I still love life. I'm in love again. Just got married for the third time and going strong."

Beautiful, stately Faye, age seventy-four: "I don't feel like I'm seventy-four. I'm not even sure that I am seventy-four. All I know is that I feel *young.* I'm still lively and active. My memory is as good as ever."

Mario, age seventy, still has a full head of gray hair and a twinkle in his eye: "My life is more thrilling today than it ever was. I'm in good health and still look at women with a young man's eye and appetite."

Martha, widowed two years, age sixty-eight and pleasingly plump: "I take risks now I never took before. I used to be so fearful of not being liked or rejected that I never said 'No' to anyone who made demands on my time—especially when I really wanted to do things for me. I can say no now without feeling like a horrible person. I'm no longer afraid of what people will think of me. I decided to be good to Martha."

James, age seventy-four: "I don't think about age—I feel ageless. I don't feel I'm too old for anything. I take courses in adult education, I dance four times a week, I go on picnics with my grandchildren, I'm having a ball."

Ethel, age sixty-seven: "I don't pay attention to my aches and pains. I'm involved and in love with life. I do what I can and enjoy it immensely. I have no time to worry about old age."

I can't list all the comments—that would make a book in itself. Suffice it to say, there are many people in advanced years who are ignoring their calendar years. There were some, however, who admitted they felt *older* than they actually are. For example, Muriel, a widow, age fifty, said, "I feel like a hundred. I'm so bored. There's nothing to get up for in the morning except to go out to the pool." Muriel is bored because she doesn't put forth any effort to get out of the rut she's in. And only *she* can do it. She sits around the pool all day with an attitude that says, "Come on life, bring me some happiness, bring me some excitement." She is waiting for something to "happen." Instead of *making* things happen, she sits and wallows in self-pity. Life is *not* going to knock on her door and say, "Hi, are you Muriel? I've come to make you happy. I brought you some nice men, some interesting hobbies . . . You just sit and sun yourself . . . I will bring the excitement to you."

Life gives you *nothing*. Life just offers you the *opportunity* to create your own destiny; to create your own excitement; to improve; to go forward. Life says, "If you want to be happy in this world, get off your fanny and look for the circumstances you want. If you can't find them, create your own happenings." Muriel has to stop committing "psychological suicide" and come to the realization that to get out of a rut is a do-it-yourself task.

I just saw the play *Our Town* on television again the other day. If you recall the play, one of the characters dies and wants to come back to earth for one more day. She is granted this request. Back on earth she remarks, "Oh, you good earth—does a human being realize what it means to be alive?" Do we really realize what it means to be alive? Dare to live! Dare to do! Don't worry about your chronological age. A new life will begin for you when you let it begin. Don't waste time—it's too precious. Take a chance. Build up an immunity to fear by *doing* the things you fear to do. Don't try to be perfect. Just live! To live is to be imperfect. The person who never makes a mistake is either actually dead or living the life of a human vegetable.

PSYCHOLOGICAL VITAMINS CAN HELP YOU ENJOY LIFE

Many of us are familiar with the vitamins that are manufactured in the laboratory, but the kind of vitamins I'm talking about right now cannot be bought anywhere because they are manufactured in your own mind. No matter what your problem may be, there is a psychological vitamin to help lift up your spirits and give you the mental and physical strength to carry on. Live one day at a time and use the "vitamins" as you need them.

When things are not going well for you and everything seems bleak, don't despair. Use the psychological vitamins to pull you through.

Let's start with vitamin A. Have you made a mistake and do you feel miserable as a result? *Accept* yourself and like yourself in spite of it. You are not perfect. Are you timid? Did you buy some merchandise you can't use and won't return it because you are ashamed to do so? *Assert* yourself. Take it back—nothing will happen to you. Did the waiter bring you cold, well-done roast beef when you ordered hot, rare roast beef? Assert yourself—send it back.

Did you have a rough day yesterday? Take your psychological vitamin B and make today a *better* day. Make it a *beautiful* day.

Do you feel nervous, anxious, or fearful today? Use all the vitamin Cs you can think of. Tell yourself you are getting *calmer* by the minute. Tell yourself you are *courageous, confident, composed,* over and over again.

Are you easily upset, irritated? When you awaken in the morning tell yourself, "I'm going to make today a *delightful* day—nothing and no one can upset me."

One of my students, a very lively widow of sixty-two, told the class she uses the vitamin D to make herself more *desir-*

able when she has a date. "I tell myself," she said, "I'm going to look and act desirable and it spurs me on to look good and act feminine.

Do you feel listless? Lethargic? Use all the vitamin Es you can think of. Make yourself *enthusiastic* about something. You need enthusiasm for energy. Your spirits will be elevated when you put all the Es into action. A and E mix well together. In fact, all the psychological vitamins are to be taken together just as we take all the biological vitamins together.

We come now to the most important psychological vitamin—Vitamin F. Be *free!* Free yourself of guilt feelings, free yourself of negative attitudes, free yourself of fears, be free to live the way *you* want to live and not the way others say you should live.

I'm sure you get the message. All those psychological vitamins are manufactured in your own mind. If you use them you will enjoy life. Nothing can defeat you—no problem will wear you out.

YOU DON'T "LOSE" YOUR MEMORY

Memory loss is due mostly to lazy habits—it is not a sign of old age. There is no age limit on memory. Many studies have been made on what happens to memory as we grow older and it was found that those who exercised their memories had no problems as they grew older. Memory is a matter of training. As I stated earlier, if you force yourself to think, to learn new things, to memorize, the better your memory will be. If you keep telling yourself, "I have a rotten memory" or "I am getting old—my memory is failing," you will go downhill.

Intellectual decline is due more to poor health or laziness

than to age. I read just the other day in one of the newspapers that a man of eighty-seven and a woman of eighty had earned their bachelor's degrees. They are average people like you and me. They decided they wanted a college degree so they worked at getting it.

Deterioration of memory is *not* part of the aging process. You don't have to be "old" to bury painful or unpleasant experiences. The young do this also. Sometimes repression of very painful experiences is necessary for survival. For example, if women didn't repress their memories of labor pains, they would never have more than one child. I remember I was in labor a long time with my first child. I had a doctor who believed in natural childbirth (only he didn't tell me that at the time). While I was in labor he did nothing to help me. I hated him; I vowed I would never have another child. Several years later I wanted another child. I forgot the actual pain—it was repressed—but I remembered the long labor so I asked the second doctor not to let me suffer. Little did I know even then that he, too, would do nothing to help me when the time came. I was in labor long with my second child, too. But I can't remember the actual *pain* now. Natural childbirth is easier today—there are exercises to do that make it much better. I wasn't aware of the techniques then and neither were my doctors. The point I'm making is that many kinds of painful or unpleasant experiences are forgotten and it's all to the good. Some of us need a course in forgetting rather than in memory. Yesterday is over—it's finished, gone—it no longer exists unless you keep it alive by constantly reliving it.

At any rate, the studies on memory are consistent. The more you use it, the longer you have it, and the better it is. Most of the scientific evidence indicates that mental performance may even improve with age. If the mind is stimulated, we can continue to learn as long as we live; memory has no age limits at all.

How to Improve Your Physical Health

4

Health is so necessary to all the duties as well as pleasures of life, that the crime of squandering it is equal to the folly.

Samuel Johnson

At what level is your health now? How do you feel when you wake up? Are you refreshed? Fatigued? Raring to go? Are you in good health, fair or mediocre health, or ill health? If you have neglected your physical health, you *can* improve it and even turn back your biological age quite a number of years through optimum nutrition and exercise. Maintaining a healthy body is something you have to do every day. At no time can you afford to neglect or ignore your health—especially now past fifty. What you want is optimum health, not mediocre health. Many people are aging prematurely because of inadequate nutrition. They may even be overweight, but malnourished. With a high intake of nutrients you can achieve maximum health for your body.

Believe that you can revitalize your tissues and organs and be rejuvenated internally with the proper food. This will bring about renewed youth and vigor. You have to be rejuvenated psychologically *and* physically for optimum health. Physical and psychological health are interdependent. For example, if you eat something that disagrees with you—you may have heartburn or indigestion or you may feel bloated; and it will affect you psychologically as well. You may become irritable, snap at people (even at those you love), be moody or hard to get along with. The physiological affects the psychological and the psychological affects the physiological. On the other hand, if your attitudes are negative, if you are very emotional—upset, anxious, tense—worry constantly, are fearful and full of hostilities, then ingesting all the wonderful nutrients and vitamins in the world will be a waste. You are poisoning your body with your attitudes and emotions, which may lead to all kinds of illnesses. So even though I am stressing good nutrition now as a most important factor in optimum health (and I'm a great believer in vitamins and good nutrition), I have to say: First you are what you *think,* second, what you *eat.* You cannot beat this combination, especially when you add some exercise to it, too.

WHAT GOOD NUTRITION HAS DONE FOR ME

I am what is termed a "health nut." So are many television and film stars—they must stay youthful as long as possible. I am healthier today in my fifties than I was in my youth. I am stronger, more vigorous, can work longer hours, and I *feel* younger today than twenty-five years ago. My body is younger, too. I firmly believe that a positive, optimistic approach to life, the ability to cope with stressful situations, a high regard for physical health, and a proper diet can delay the aging process for a long time.

Psychology is my field but since the mind and body are connected I studied nutrition, too. When I began to eat "live" food as opposed to "dead" food (junk food) I noticed a change in my skin. It began to look better and better, smoother and smoother. My nails and hair grew very fast, also. I must confess that at one time, many years ago, I couldn't let a day go by without consuming large quantities of cake, candy, commercial ice cream and all the junk food you can possibly think of. I didn't have a weight problem (I was careful to eat less of anything else), I just had pimples. The most I weighed was 135 pounds (I'm 5 feet 7 1/2 inches). As soon as I began to study nutrition and learned (among other things) how deleterious sugar and salt are to the body, I cured myself of my addiction to junk food with autosuggestion. I told myself that I hated cake, candy, and ice cream, over and over again. I told myself it was *poison*. It took one month to cure myself of the habit. After that I no longer felt frustrated or irritable if I didn't have the junk food. In fact, I no longer craved it—I could look at it and not desire it. When I passed a bakery store I didn't see cake and cookies; I saw poison.

Ninety percent of my diet is *raw*. I live mostly on a high-fiber diet: fresh fruits and raw vegetables, nuts, seeds, whole grains, baked potatoes. I'm not completely vegetarian. I eat fish and chicken once in a while, and sometimes broiled chicken livers with whole-grain brown rice. When I go out on a date, I fortify myself at home first. I have some yogurt or fresh fruit or nuts and order very little in the restaurant. Just broiled fish or broiled chicken with a baked potato. I have been told that I'm a "cheap date." No drinks, no dessert—just the main course. Of course, my date doesn't know that I have already taken the edge off my hunger at home so that I can afford to eat sparingly in the restaurant. While he has a drink, I have Perrier water (or any other bottled water) and I can wait for the main course without partaking of bread and butter.

I believe in eggs because they are a complete protein food. I eat an egg every day. There have been many studies made regarding eggs and cholesterol. The studies concluded that eggs do not raise one's cholesterol. The egg yolk contains choline (one of the B vitamins) and lecithin, which help to emulsify cholesterol in the body and not deposit it in the walls of the arteries. My cholesterol today is lower than it ever was. I attribute it to the kinds of foods I eat and the way I eat. I also lost ten pounds eating my way. I like being slimmer, I feel more energetic. I consume most of my calories at breakfast. (Not all healthful food is low in calories.) I can go for hours without a slump in energy. Also, eating most of my calories at breakfast gives me all day to work them off. I never permit myself to get too hungry—that's why I carry snacks (nuts, seeds, etc.) in my handbag in case I want something to nibble on. Dinner is never too hearty.

I try to eat an early dinner so that many hours elapse between dinner and bedtime. That, too, helps to keep the weight down. I just have an apple or half a cup of yogurt an hour before bedtime. You should not go to bed hungry because you may not be able to sleep. It is a good idea to have some milk or yogurt before you go to bed, as the calcium in yogurt and milk induces sleep.

The less we eat over fifty the better off we are. I have trained myself to *undereat* rather than overeat. In case my readers are curious, yes, I do eat brewer's yeast and bran, and take lots of vitamins. I mix yeast, bran, whole-grain cereal, lecithin, almonds and walnuts together for breakfast with a glass of milk and a banana added. Wow! Delicious, too.

What is good for me may not be good for someone else so I suggest that you take your doctor's advice if you have any kind of health problem. Many of my students in their sixties and seventies have benefited from my suggestions on nutrition but I know them, and since I don't know you, I can't say what *you* should eat. I can safely say, however, that *live* food can only do you good, not harm, and that junk food contributes nothing to your body or well-being.

WHAT GOOD NUTRITION CAN DO FOR YOU—NOW—PAST FIFTY

My intention is not to discuss the various diets now in vogue, but rather the general principles of nutrition and eating habits which will maximize your physical health. After you have finished reading the entire chapter you can plan your own program for optimum physical health, because in the long run it is you who must take the responsibility to preserve your health and lengthen your life. We all have the power to do so.

Let's not trade health for the pleasure of eating food that is nutritionally useless. It isn't worth it. It is easier to prevent a disease than to cure it. Sound nutrition will supply you with all the nutrients necessary for maintaining health *without gaining weight.* As you grow older you may not be as active physically, which means less food is needed. If you overeat, it will be deposited as fatty tissue. If you get fat from too much sugar, starchy foods, and too much alcohol, your health may suffer from the lack of sufficient roughage, vitamins, and minerals. Your bodily resistance to disease may be lowered, too. Inadequate nutrition is an important factor in aging prematurely. With the proper nutrients and good eating habits, plus some vitamins, the aging process *can* be reversed. A fad diet may cause you to lose weight quickly, but it is not desirable for good health. With proper nourishment—optimal nutrition *every day*—you can lose and keep it off. We all require the same nutrients, but in different amounts. Some need more, others need less. That's why you must create your own optimum health program. If you are under a great deal of stress, you need *more* nutrients than someone who leads a very calm, relaxed life. Stress is a thief—it robs your body of the B vitamins and vitamin C. Your body is the final judge.

Perhaps some of you are thinking, "But I'm too old now

to change my dietary habits—it's too late." Oh no, it isn't! *It's never too late.* Begin today to undo the damage that has been done. As soon as you put into your body good, nourishing food, and chew it well so that it will be absorbed into the bloodstream, excellent nutrition has begun. With determination, you can make your body stronger through high quality nutrition and exercise.

There are some people who don't want to do anything about their habits of eating. Neither do they want to get well. For example, one day in a lecture on self-destructiveness I indicated that if one eats food that is deleterious to his medical condition (for example, too much salt when one has high blood pressure or heart disease), it is self-destructive. A tall, heavy-set man stood up and argued the point with me. He was a new student; I didn't even know his name. "How could you say such a thing?" he shouted. "I know I'm not supposed to have salt—I have a heart condition. Even when I leave my doctor's office after he's told me not to have salt, I go right across the street to this wonderful deli and I have a hot pastrami sandwich with loads of pickles and I feel absolutely marvelous. I enjoy every mouthful. I'm having a ball and *you* tell me that's self-destructive?" "Yes, sir," I said. "You are destroying yourself. I am merely offering unconscious reasons for self-destruction, but please listen to your medical doctor or your lungs will fill up with water." At the next class, I was informed that he was in the hospital—his lungs had filled up with water. Three weeks later he came back to class and said, "I'm sorry. I had a lot of time to think things over in the hospital. I didn't understand what you meant by self-destructive behavior. I would like to learn how to change my eating habits first."

There are others who say, "Neglect myself? Not me!" Here's a partial list of junk foods they eat and drink:

Coffee
Tea
Sugared foods

- Pickled foods
- Smoked foods
- Highly salted foods
- Soft drinks—especially cola drinks
- Alcohol
- Processed foods
- Fatty meats
- Potato chips
- Doughnuts and cakes
- Ice cream
- Candy

The list is endless. And when they go into a restaurant they say to the waiter, in effect, "Poison me as quickly as you can." So the waiter brings them devitalized white rolls and bread, pickled cucumbers doctored up with preservatives, a platter of corned beef, salami, and other well-doctored meats. "I want some more poison, please, waiter." So the waiter brings a bottle of soda (more carbon dioxide). And finally, they say, "Come on now, waiter, that's not enough poison—bring me pie à la mode and hot coffee." And their stomachs blow hot and cold at the same time. No wonder some people have so many diseases and age prematurely.

Suppose you ate the following nutritious foods instead; you would slow down the aging process and have a healthier body chemistry:

- All fresh fruits and all kinds of raw vegetables. (Wash them well in a solution called "Heavenly Horsetail." It's a cleanser for fruits and vegetables; it removes the pesticides and fungicides and is *safe* and *natural.*
- Baked potatoes with skins on.
- 100 percent stone ground whole-wheat bread (if you need bread).
- Unrefined carbohydrates such as oats, buckwheat, barley, brown rice, lentils, nuts, sunflower seeds, pumpkin seeds, millet, soybeans, and other beans.
- Brewer's yeast (very important for the nervous system).

Chicken.
Fish (not too much—there's too much mercury).
Low-fat cottage cheese.
Yogurt.
Eggs.
Olive oil (good lubricant for the intestines besides containing essential fatty acids).
Postum (instead of coffee) or rose hip tea (no caffeine).
Vitamin and mineral supplements.

I don't own a health food store. I don't get a piece of the action from any vitamin company. I'm suggesting vitamins because I take them and most of the studies in nutrition recommend them. Here, too, it depends on the individual as to how much he or she should take. Even if you take only what the labels on the bottles of vitamins indicate (which is not enough for some people), it would be better than nothing.

But we *do* need some vitamin supplements because even the best natural, wholesome diet may not meet all of our nutritional needs. Besides, we can't always get a "balanced" diet. Many of us don't eat too much—and as we get older the less we eat the better—so we have to supplement our diet with vitamins and minerals. Also, the older we get, the more calcium we need to prevent brittle bones. If you can't drink milk, a good source is a chelated calcium and magnesium combination.

Since this is *not* a book on nutrition, I would like to sum up with the following tips:

- You *can* improve your health after fifty. Nearly all disease has an emotional component and a nutritional component. To better your health you have to treat *both*.
- Eat live foods to stay young.
- Vitamins are preventive medicine.
- Don't buy wilted or anemic-looking vegetables.

- Don't eat "dead" foods (junk food does not provide for optimum health).
- Let your body be the final judge. If something doesn't agree with you, nutritious or not, don't eat it.
- Throw out your sugar bowl and salt shaker.
- Don't buy processed food (it's devitalized—contains calories but no nutrients).
- Eat a nourishing breakfast and you will have constant energy for several hours.
- Read labels when marketing—watch out for chemicals and preservatives.
- Try not to eat too many foods that contain preservatives or chemicals—the body can filter out only so much poison.
- Above all, don't become neurotic about food! You're not going to find 100 percent "pure" food anywhere. But at least you don't have to add more poison knowingly.
- Eat as many raw vegetables as you can. Raw vegetables are full of nutrients, high fiber, and enzymes. An enzyme stimulates chemical changes in the body. It acts as a catalyst. If you cook vegetables, the enzymes are destroyed. Enzymes are a built-in fountain of youth.
- Eat other high-roughage foods (they alleviate constipation and are good for your colon) such as whole-grain products, bran, rolled oats, brown rice, nuts, fresh fruits (washed well).
- One or two cups of coffee a day probably won't harm you, but if you are a coffee addict—if you drink six or more cups a day—beware. The caffeine in all that coffee may bring on any number of ailments, even low blood

sugar. There is ample evidence that coffee aggravates high blood pressure and coronary disease. It's an unnecessary stimulant for anyone with heart disease and doctors often forbid patients to drink coffee. The more coffee you drink the greater your need for a "pick-up." It lifts you up and then knocks you down. Caffeine also causes a vitamin B loss. Wean yourself *away* from coffee and you will be surprised to find that you are less nervous and less fatigued. Black coffee causes greater stimulation of gastric secretions than any other beverage—it aggravates ulcers. Incidentally, if you do drink an occasional cup of coffee, don't add sugar. Sugar robs the body of the B vitamins and only adds empty calories to the body.

HOW TO LOSE WEIGHT EASILY AND KEEP IT OFF

If you haven't been successful in losing weight or in keeping it off, try dieting "psychologically." That's the only way *any* diet will work for you. You might even tell yourself, "I am going to eat sensibly—I'm going to change my eating habits," instead of, "I'm going on a diet." The word *diet* in itself denotes deprivation for some people and they begin to feel sorry for themselves or become frustrated and irritable. Husbands have told me they would rather their wives remain fat then go on a diet—they become so grouchy and irritable while dieting. I have heard the same thing from wives about their husbands.

In order to fight weight gain, first you have to know the difference between appetite and hunger. Appetite is desire.

It is a psychological desire to eat for pleasure. It has to do with taste and the appearance of food. In fact, appetite is strictly a psychological factor which means that you can control it by sending a message to your brain. If you are upset about something or have heard some unpleasant news, you may be sending a message to your brain such as, "I can't eat now—I'm too upset—I can't swallow food." And you probably will not be able to eat. On the other hand, if you are upset and you are in the *habit* of eating when you are frustrated or worried, you will be sending a different message to your brain, such as, "I must have some chocolate cake with a scoop of ice cream. I'll feel better. After all, what else have I got in life?" If as a child you were soothed by your mother when you were "hurting" (either emotionally or physically) with certain foods or a second helping of cake or ice cream or a piece of candy, now, as an adult, you will be in the habit of comforting yourself with food when you are upset.

Losing weight has a lot to do with habit. Habits are powerful—they control us. However, habits can be changed and eating habits most certainly can be changed.

Hunger is physiological. It is associated with contractions of the stomach. Hunger is painful and unpleasant. If you permit your blood sugar to drop too low (because you didn't eat breakfast or haven't eaten anything for many hours), you do need food. It is more desirable to keep your blood sugar up by having small snacks *every two hours or so*. Eat an apple, or a few nuts (seven or eight), or a small banana, or a little buttermilk, or a small piece of cheese. If you work, you can carry your snacks in a plastic bag and get a thermos bottle for buttermilk or pure water. This will *not* put weight on you—in fact, you will never be too hungry so you won't have to overeat. Having healthful snacks also takes care of the desire to have something in your mouth all the time. There are some people who are constantly eating, but eating the wrong kind of food. To satisfy their desire for food they eat candy or cake or pretzels. You should eat often, but eat the *right* kind of snacks. You can also refrain from eating too much by talking a lot. The mouth doesn't care—as long as it is moving. Men who have a cigar in their mouths at all times (unlit) have to have something in their mouths. They have to chew on something to relieve tension. Pleasure is pleasure, whether it's chain-smoking or eating constantly or talking incessantly. There's no doubt that overeating is more psychological than physiological. Public speaking, incidentally, can help you to lose weight, too. Many speakers do not eat before making a speech and after the speech they are so "high" that the desire for food is curbed. So it is with performers, too. It is said, "Full stomach, empty brain." The stomach has to draw blood from the brain to digest the food. Get involved in speech-making and don't eat before the speech. You may not even desire food afterward. If you are one of the speakers at a banquet and sitting on the dais, nibble at the food. Not only will you lose weight but you will be more effective.

Nervousness, restlessness, boredom, insecurity, frustration, disappointment, discouragement, tension; these are the devils that cause you to overeat. Food acts as a sedative. You are soothed for the moment. Then there are some people who overeat because they may have no other sources of pleasure. As one of my overweight students said, "What else have I got in life?" She eats not because her body is crying out for food, but rather for love, affection, approval, acceptance, and emotional security.

Gnawing hunger is not genuine hunger but a symptom that something is wrong in your emotional life. You are seeking relief from your nervousness or uneasiness. Overeating is a form of intoxication. As we grow older, we have to reduce our food intake because our powers of digestion are not the same as they were when we were much younger. If you eat within your digestive limitations, your digestion will be good and the wholesome food you ingest will be assimilated properly.

The pleasure of eating comes from chewing well, which enhances the flavor of the food. Eating more slowly and chewing longer helps to control your intake of food. You fill up faster. Digestion begins in the mouth. By expending your energy in chewing *long* and *leisurely,* you will also burn up calories. If you are very busy, don't eat; you will be training yourself to endure hunger. Drink water instead. However, always have something in your handbag, coat pocket, or, if you are a working person, in your office. When you find a little time to relax, have a snack. Little snacks, as I indicated earlier, keep your blood sugar up. You will have constant energy and lose weight at the same time. I eat my banana leisurely in the car as I am driving from one place to another. I may have some nuts or an apple other times. As a result, I have constant energy. If you gobble down a hearty lunch, you won't be mentally alert if you have to engage in heavy mental work immediately afterward. You will feel more like napping than working.

You can lose weight *without even trying.* I would like you to think in terms of *health*—not dieting—so you won't feel like you are depriving yourself of goodies. Losing weight and keeping it off is a skill that can be acquired like any other skill. When you say with conviction, "I am the master of my appetite," you will develop a feeling of power. Don't listen to anyone who says to you, "Just taste it," or "Just have one piece of chocolate or one pretzel." You may not be hungry at the time, but as soon as you have aroused your taste buds, you may not stop at one piece. The brain stirs up the appetite.

Psychological influences may increase or decrease your hunger. When you feel hunger after you have eaten a substantial meal, ask yourself, "Is it really physical hunger? Does my *stomach* want food or am I hungry for stimulation, for excitement, for affection?" Examine your hunger, write down what you ate, and then ask yourself, "How is it possible to be hungry again after all that food I ingested a short time ago? No, it must be psychological hunger—now what am I going to do about it? What can I do to stop this gnawing sensation?" *You can do a lot.* Bear in mind that appetite is not prudent. It is pure desire—a craving for food when there is no physiological need for food. Each time you yield to appetite, your cravings are strengthened. You become a slave to your appetite. You are not a free person. Start doing something immediately to divert your attention from food.

The following tips will help you to lose weight and stay slim:

- Try on the clothes that no longer fit you. Hang them up outside the closet door and leave them there so that you can see them every day. Tell yourself, "By golly, I'm going to fit into those clothes again—I am determined." Or buy a beautiful dress or suit a size smaller and tell yourself the same thing.
- Motivate yourself. *Desire* is the answer. You must have a burning desire to lose weight and keep it off. You must love yourself enough not only to want to look good, but to be *healthy*. Motivate yourself by looking forward to a reward when you lose the amount of weight you have set for yourself. A reward can be anything: a cruise, a trip, a new wardrobe (depending on your financial status), or just one particular outfit you didn't dare to wear because you were too heavy. Your long-term reward, however, will be better health and a longer life.
- When the craving for food reappears, distract yourself. Talk to someone on the phone who is stimulating. As long as your mouth is moving you can control the craving. Take a walk and tell yourself silently with conviction, "I

want to be slim; I love being slim; I shall lose the weight." And as you are walking, see yourself in your mind's eye as a slim person. Have a picture in your mind of how you want to look. Your unconscious will strive for realization of your goal.
- Drink a glass of water five minutes *before* each meal. It will curb your hunger. Drink water *between* meals to curb hunger also.
- Use mental weapons to combat the longing for high-calorie foods or junk food. Be so busy that you don't have time to think about food. Become so absorbed in life, in finding ways to feed your emotional hunger, that you won't live just to eat.
- If you are in the habit of eating while watching television, you have two choices: (1) Don't watch television—become absorbed in something else. (2) If you do decide to watch television, when you feel the urge to eat, go into the bathroom, sit down on the toilet seat in the dark, and eat. Pretty soon it will be revolting to you and you will break the habit of eating while watching television. (One of my clients asked me, "How will you know if I eat in the toilet?" "I'll know," I said. "You will lose weight because you will get damn tired of running back and forth to the toilet and you will come to the realization that you are only fooling yourself, not me . . . unless you enjoy eating in the dark on a toilet seat. In that case, we will use another mental weapon. Use your imagination and visualize poison all over the food that you shouldn't have, such as cake, ice cream, etc. If your imagination is strong enough you *won't* be able to eat that

junk food." This method worked for her. She lost twenty pounds.)
- You can control your appetite much better throughout the day if you start with a good breakfast.
- If you are a night eater and consume a great deal of food at night because of loneliness or boredom, send a message to your brain that you have had enough food for today (there is an appetite center located at the base of the brain).
- If you are truly hungry (physically hungry) at bedtime, have an apple or an orange or some plain yogurt—you will sleep better.
- If you get an urge to eat when you have already had enough nourishment for the day, keep looking at the dress or trousers you want to fit into.
- Stay away from "appetite inciters" such as condiments, salt, pepper, alcohol.
- Eat mostly high-fiber foods. You fill up quicker from the bulk (fruits, raw vegetables, whole grains).
- Keep sending messages to your brain after each light meal: "I am full—I have had enough."
- Avoid caffeine—no coffee, tea, cocoa, or cola drinks. Drink *water!* Not *with* meals—before meals.
- Baked potatoes are *not* fattening. Eat a small one almost every day. It is filling. Combined with low-fat cottage cheese, it's a complete meal.
- Don't use food to compensate for your frustrations. Learn to take frustration. It's not so terrible if you think right.

- If the doctor who is treating you for obesity is fat, find another doctor.
- You can lose weight steadily *without even trying*. Learn how to cope with boredom and disappointment—find outlets other than food.
- Don't weaken—don't have even an occasional taste of pie, cake, or any sugared foods. *Reeducate your eating habits.* As an analogy, a surgeon doesn't cut out a piece of the cancer—he cuts it *all out*. It's the same with smoking. You don't cut down to five or six cigarettes a day—you cut it all out. You don't have a piece of cake or ice cream when you are frustrated—you cut it *all out*. I am stressing this because if you are terribly frustrated or disappointed one day, you will not stop at one piece of candy or one piece of cake or any other junk food—you will undo what you have started. If your taste buds are reeducated and your emotions and attitudes are reeducated, you will turn to other outlets rather than to food. *All the food in the world will not satisfy your emotional hunger.* But some kind of positive action will help—even a change in attitude toward the situation or person.
- Don't feel sorry for yourself—you are not "dieting." You are eating sensibly. You are working toward optimum health and you will lose weight automatically.
- Finally, you can either remain plump or lose weight. The decision is yours. If you are happy with yourself as you are, plump and overweight, fine, then be happy—but be good and happy both consciously *and* uncon-

sciously. Don't hate yourself unconsciously when you go shopping for clothes. In fact, don't hate yourself at all. Just learn to distinguish real hunger from emotional hunger so that you don't go too far in terms of "plumpness."

There's a story circulating around Miami Beach about a very fat lady who boarded a crowded bus and managed to squeeze herself in. She had a long way to ride and was feeling very uncomfortable (she had eaten a very hearty lunch), so she reached behind her and unzipped her skirt. A few minutes later she reached back and zipped it up again. Feeling more and more uncomfortable, however, she reached back and unzipped the zipper, but in a few minutes zipped herself up again. This went on for nearly twenty minutes until finally the man standing behind her leaned over and said, "Listen, lady, I don't know what's on your mind, but in the last twenty minutes, you've unzipped my fly at least ten times!"

There may be a message here—don't overeat.

EXERCISE IS NECESSARY TO PREVENT ATROPHY

No matter how old you are, you need some form of exercise (unless your health is so poor, your doctor forbids it). You must use your body in every way possible. If your muscles or joints are stiff, they will become worse if you don't move around. Exercise promotes circulation and nourishes the brain—even if you just take a brisk walk. *Anything* that we can do to improve general circulation will also help the brain. If your circulation is poor, the brain cells are not being nourished adequately. I'm not recommending vigorous exercise for people in advanced years unless they have been exercising all their lives. Mild exercise (if your doctor permits it) in the form of stretching, bending, walking *every day* is all that is needed to prevent atrophy and benefit impaired circulation.

Walking strengthens the heart and promotes flexibility of the joints. Resting too much does more harm than good. We need movement. If you have not used your muscles for years, they have grown weak from disuse. Exercise will strengthen them. You will feel better and look better, too, due to improved circulation. The more we rest the more calcium we lose from our bones, which in turn weakens them. Physical activity prevents this loss. You have to move your joints to keep them mobile.

When I take a brisk walk after I have been sitting for some time (teaching or writing), I feel fantastic. In fact, when I'm writing I try not to sit for too long a period. I break it up with stretching, standing, or walking around my apartment for a few minutes every hour or so. When I'm talking on the phone I deliberately walk around the room (I have a long cord).

If you are a working person and sit at your desk all day, take a "walking break" instead of a coffee break. Walk all around your office for at least five minutes, briskly. Try to stand up as much as possible.

If you are home, look for opportunities to stand up. If you watch television, every time there's a commercial stand up and stretch or walk around. Only don't walk in the direction of the refrigerator—walk the other way.

The following tips are worth keeping in mind:

- Given a choice between a movie and dancing, choose dancing. It's great exercise for people in advanced years. You move every muscle when you dance.

- Wear comfortable shoes when walking for *exercise*. The effects of wearing uncomfortable shoes (for style) are many (calluses, bunions, corns, etc.). Wearing very high, fashionable heels for walking is bad for your back. Very high heels are "sitting" shoes.
- Take long strides when walking (but not too long for your body—you be the judge).
- Remind yourself a few times a day to straighten up, whether you are walking, sitting, or standing. Pull in your stomach and keep your rib cage elevated until it becomes a habit. People with good posture seldom suffer back problems. Always keep your back straight.
- When sitting, move around in your chair—change your position from time to time.
- If you can, walk up a few flights of stairs instead of using the elevator. Also walk down.
- Do not overexert yourself at a given time if you are not in good condition. Do a little more each day.
- When you take a long walk for exercise it should be uninterrupted. Don't stop and window shop—that is not exercise. It has to be continuous movement for at least one hour. If you feel tired after a brisk walk of a few miles, it's natural. Walk for one half hour instead and gradually work up to one hour.
- When you are doing tasks at home try doing them standing up and moving around rather than sitting.
- Lie on your back on the floor (no pillow), pick up your feet, and allow your ankles to rest on the seat of a chair. If you have been sitting a lot, this will reverse the circulation so your

blood flows to your head. Do this a few times a day for five or ten minutes at a time if you sit a lot.
- Do not walk in hot sun. Walk in your home. Walk in the lobby of your building. Walk up and down the corridor. As long as you keep moving you will increase your agility.
- Do not take a brisk walk after eating a hearty meal (too much strain on the heart). Some people say, "I feel so full, I must take a walk." That's the worst thing you can do. Sit still and rest if you are too full. (To eat that much can be hazardous to your health and life.) Also, if you go out dining and dancing, either dance all you want *before* you eat or wait at least forty-five minutes *after* you eat to dance. Not only is it bad for your digestive tract to dance too soon after eating, but it also causes too much strain on the heart. I see middle-aged and older people dancing between courses or immediately after they are through eating. This is dangerous. I was never able to do this even when I was very young. I used to get a stomach ache if I danced with a lot of food in my stomach. Some people can do this and feel nothing, but it is a strain on the heart.

One of my students is eighty years old and has a heart condition. He told me that his doctor told him he could dance all night, but on an *empty* stomach. He went to a New Year's Eve party but he had his dinner at five o'clock at home. He wasn't interested in the food—just in the people, dancing, and having fun. He outdanced everyone and felt terrific. Others who were younger than he felt sluggish and couldn't keep up with him. I might add that sexual activity is also a form of exercise and should be engaged in on an *empty* stomach. Eat *afterward*—or wait at least two hours after dinner. One of my clients, a man of sixty, told me he got indigestion every time he indulged in sexual activity immediately after a meal. It didn't bother his girl friend, who was much younger than he. However, I know many younger people who cannot have sex either on full stomachs.

- Be your own doctor. Try various exercises, walking briskly (slowly at first, then increasing the pace). If you feel you are exerting yourself too much, go at a slower pace, but don't stop moving around.

How to Handle Problems with Your Family

5

YOUR RELATIONSHIP WITH YOUR DAUGHTER-IN-LAW

"I can't get along with my daughter-in-law," Estelle told me in a counseling session. "I always wanted a daughter—but she is so cold and unfriendly, I'm very unhappy." It would be nice if her daughter-in-law were warmer and friendlier, but the fact that she isn't does not mean that Estelle cannot be happy. It has nothing to do with leading a full, exciting life and doing her own thing. Estelle had to learn that it is not the problem in itself that causes the unhappiness—it's not being able to cope that is a problem.

Let's examine some of the reasons for dissension between mother-in-law and daughter-in-law. Some mothers-in-law create their own problems. What kind of mother-in-law are you? Do you offer unasked for "constructive criticism?" Do you talk, talk, talk, when you visit until your daughter-in-law gets a headache? Do you give the impression that *your* way of running a home is better? Do you make your daughter-in-law feel inadequate by your facial expression and/or by your gestures (nonverbal language)? Have you let go of your son, or do you meddle in his life? Do you tell your daughter-in-law how to bring up your grandchildren? Do you tell her how to feed her family? Do you criticize your daughter-in-law because the dinner wasn't good, or the house not clean?

Be honest with yourself. If you can identify with some of the above causes for friction in an in-law relationship, you can do something about it. *Stop doing what you are doing.* Stop giving advice (unless asked). Stop meddling. Stay out of the kitchen unless you are invited in. Let go of your son— he's a grown man, your daughter-in-law may resent your holding on to him. Look for opportunities to compliment her. Would you criticize a friend if the dinner wasn't good, or tell her you don't like the way she runs her home? Nothing is opened by mistake more than the mouth. A friend of mine just returned from a visit with her son and daughter-in-law. She looked so dejected I couldn't help asking what was wrong. "I should have put a zipper on my mouth," she said.

If you don't like the way your daughter-in-law runs the home, say nothing (it's *their* life and *their* home). It won't do any good and can only cause resentment. Be sure, too, your face doesn't communicate disapproval. If you don't like the way she is rearing your grandchildren, that's too bad, but they are *her* children, not yours. You have to look the other way when you visit. In fact, if certain things bother you it would be desirable to keep your visits very short. Make it pleasant for *yourself*—enjoy it while you are there. Tell yourself, "I'm here—I might as well enjoy it. I have a chance to see my son and my grandchildren, and whatever my daughter-in-law says or does will not affect me in any way. I'll be nice to her in spite of her coldness."

Now let's assume you are *not* the kind of mother-in-law I just described. You don't meddle, you don't give uncalled for advice, you let go of your son a long time ago, you mind your own business, you step over the newspapers on the floor. Whatever your daughter-in-law does is fine with you —even if she serves TV dinners, your attitude is, if he's happy, that's all that matters—and your daughter-in-law still is cold and unfriendly. Now, we have to consider unconscious feelings that may be behind this coldness. You may be a threat to your daughter-in-law. She may resent you unconsciously for the following reasons:

Your *son* talks too much about you. "My mother's stew is tastier, you ought to get the recipe from my mother. She's a terrific cook."

"My mother brought *me* up okay, why don't you call my mother to find out why the baby cries so much?"

"My mother knows everything about running a home—why don't you ask her advice?"

"My mother always did it—why can't you?"

You may not even be aware that your son is saying these things to his wife. She may be building up resentment and repressing it, but it may manifest itself in her manner toward you. You might have a talk with your son (if you confront your daughter-in-law, she may feel guilty and not want to talk), and perhaps say something like this: "Do you know of any reason why Jane is not very friendly when I visit? Is there anything I say or do to provoke her?" This may or may not set him thinking about the things he tells her about you. He himself may be unaware that he is making her feel inadequate by constantly bringing you into the picture. You might even ask him outright, "Son, do you compare her cooking with mine? I know you always loved my cooking—do you tell her she can't cook as well?" Knowing your son's habits, you could also ask him, "Do you expect your wife to do the things I did for you, like picking up your clothes from the chair or floor and hanging them up? Forget it, son. She's not your mother, she's your wife. I was wrong—I spoiled you. You're a grown man now—hang up your own clothes. I'm not reprimanding you, I just want you to be happy with your wife." These are just some suggestions that may work: you'll have to tailor your questions to your own situation.

There may be other unconscious forces at work. Your

daughter-in-law may unconsciously resent her own mother, and you represent a "mother." You are the innocent scapegoat. No matter how wonderful a mother-in-law you may be, she won't like you. But that's her problem, not yours, and if you *understand* this, you will continue to be nice and gracious regardless of how cold she may be. In fact, train yourself not to be affected by her unfriendliness. She may come around eventually and realize that you are *not* her mother—or she may not. But this is something you can do *nothing* about. If you really accept this situation you will not feel hurt—you will be facing reality. On the other hand, a daughter-in-law may be so attached to her own mother that she may find it difficult to call you, a complete stranger, "Mother." Many of my students have complained to me that they feel uncomfortable and unhappy because their daughters-in-law do not call them "Mother." Here, too, you can do nothing but accept it. It does no good to insist that she call you "Mother"—either she can't or doesn't want to for unconscious reasons.

Some students have told me that they aren't called by their first names either. Their daughters-in-law converse with them in person or on the phone without calling them anything. What difference does it make? Your son did not choose the girl he married to make *you* happy—he chose the girl *he* wanted. So be happy that your son is happy. When they have children you will have a name—Grandma or Grandpa.

YOUR RELATIONSHIP WITH YOUR SON-IN-LAW

Many of the causes for dissension that I delineated in terms of a daughter-in-law can be applied to problems with a son-in-law. A daughter may talk too much about her father. "My father can do this . . . my father can do that . . . my father is so terrific," which will also build resentment in your son-in-law. Sometimes a son-in-law may dislike his mother-in-law or father-in-law because his wife has told him how badly she was treated when she was growing up (which may or may not be true). He identifies with his wife and as a result also resents his mother-in-law and father-in-law. The daughter perhaps did not like to be disciplined or punished and blew it all up out of proportion. But you, as an in-law, do not know what your daughter told your son-in-law. If your son-in-law has some unconscious antagonistic, angry emotions toward his own mother, he may transfer his anger on to you. He may not be able to show anger toward his own mother because he feels guilty about these feelings. Here again, you can do nothing to change your son-in-law's thinking. When you visit, just be polite and nice in spite of the fact that he may be very unfriendly. If you just be yourself, eventually he will recognize that his anger is *not* justified where you are concerned.

Another reason for resentment may be that your daughter spends too much time on the phone (especially if it's long distance), discussing little problems with you which should be discussed with him. He may feel that your influence on your daughter is greater than his. He feels threatened as a *man*. If your daughter is in the habit of doing that, you might suggest to her that while you appreciate her confiding in you, you feel that she should discuss the situation with her husband and that it is their decision to make (whatever it may be).

Another reason for resentment may be that a son-in-law has to blame somebody for his wife's irrational behavior at times—so *you* get it again. After all, you were chiefly responsible for bringing up your daughter, so whom is he going to blame? He forgets that no one can be mature all of the time, and that we all sometimes behave a little irrationally (he does, too, but that doesn't count).

And so, as an in-law, you have a choice: You can evaluate your problem *constructively* or *destructively*. How you think about your problem will be the deciding factor in how you will feel emotionally and how you will continue to react. The choice is yours. You do not have to be unhappy; you do not have to suffer if your daughter-in-law or son-in-law does not respond to you the way you would like them to. Incidentally, fathers-in-law do not get off scot-free either. Some fathers won't let go of their daughters. They, too, are criticized by sons-in-law. But it is the mother-in-law who usually gets it most of the time. So what are you going to do? Nothing. Be happy that you are an in-law—that you lived to see your children married, that you lived to see your grandchildren.

YOUR RELATIONSHIP WITH YOUR GROWN CHILDREN

Letting go of grown children may be very difficult for some parents. Somehow it seems to be easier for a father to let go than a mother. It may be that she no longer feels needed. Healthy, grown-up children want to be on their own. This indicates security and self-confidence. However, some parents impede their children's growth, like the mother who becomes ill when her son tells her he wants to get married. ("What's your hurry, son, you're only forty-eight.") Some mothers have invested too heavily in their children to the point of excluding all other interests, and these women suffer greatly when their grown children want to move away or get married. Some may even develop all kinds of psychosomatic illnesses to bring back their children. But this need not be so. When your grown children leave you for a life of their own, you can begin to live a new life. You can do the things you never had time to do.

Above all, try not to make your grown children feel guilty the way Maxine does: "Why didn't you call me for two weeks? You forgot you have a little old mother living in Florida?" This "little old mother" is living it up plenty. Busy every day—running here, there, having a ball. But if one day Maxine has nothing to do and feels bored, she lets it out on her children.

Lucille nags her daughter (who is living happily in another state) every opportunity she gets. "When are you getting married? Why don't you want to get married? When will you make me a grandmother, you're almost thirty?" When her daughter answers, understandably, "Get off my back, Mom, this is *my* life," Lucille justifies her nagging with, "But I only want you to be happy, darling." Lucille would have a much better relationship with her daughter if she looked upon her as a person who has the right to live her life the way *she* chooses. She may have built up a very interesting and fulfilling life for herself and may be quite happy being single. Lucille is really thinking about her own happiness. All of her friends' daughters are married and have children. She is jealous. She has to find some absorbing interests and make a life for herself and stop depending on her daughter to make her happy. It is easier to let go when you have a life of your own to lead.

While it is true that some daughters do not marry because they are overly attached to their fathers, others do marry and have an internal struggle. "Who comes first—daddy or my husband?" If the daughter runs home to daddy every time she has a quarrel with her husband, some professional help may be needed to break away from daddy. It's never a one-way street. Daddy may also be overly attached to his daughter. Usually, the parents' relationship with each other suffers under these circumstances. A mother may become jealous of her daughter because of the overattachment.

A son may also be overly attached to his mother, and consult his mother about everything instead of his wife. Although he may love both women, his mother seems to come first. His relationship with his wife suffers, because after a while the wife begins to resent her husband *and* her mother-in-law. Again, professional help may be required to break away from mommy if the parties concerned do not have the psychological insight nor the courage to break away. Mothers who do not have husbands to love anymore must find other people to love so that they can let go of their children.

This reminds me of the story of the young Jewish man who phoned his mother from another state to inform her that he was about to marry a Catholic girl. He was surprised that his mother didn't rant and rave and carry on, as was her pattern when he did something she didn't approve of. The mother congratulated her son, which made him more suspicious. She then suggested that they come back and live in her apartment after the honeymoon. The son said, "But, Mom, you have only one bedroom." And the mother answered, "So what? You won't need two bedrooms. After I kill myself, the two of you will be living here by yourselves."

We may love our children very much and they may love us very much, but we must let them grow and lead their own lives. A "consuming" parental love is unhealthy for all concerned. Developing our own private lives keeps us vital and youthful.

If you want a good relationship with your grown children, give them unconditional love—"I love you for what you are. Please yourself." Conditional love says, "If you do what I want you to do, if you please *me,* I will love you." No person, whether child or husband or wife, truly feels loved where conditional love exists.

If your married children are having a quarrel with their mates, try not to take sides, try not to play referee. If you do, *you* may become the enemy. If your daughter calls you up and tells you that she is miserable—she just had a terrible quarrel with her husband and wants a divorce—just listen. Let her get out her anger. You might indicate that you understand how she feels and continue to listen, rather than say anything that may backfire later on. Above all, do *not* take it so seriously that *you* become a nervous wreck and don't sleep all night. Take a "Let's see what happens" approach. They may patch it up the same evening, go to bed and make love all night, while you are crying your eyes out because she wants a divorce. Your daughter isn't going to call you up at three in the morning and say, "Wow, did we make up—I'm having a ball in bed!" She may call you the next day to let you know all is well. And she may not. She may have gotten it out of her system when you listened so intently and then forgotten about calling you back. It isn't that she means to worry you—she figures if you don't hear from her you will *know* that everything is fine, because mothers are supposed to be mindreaders, too, among other things.

YOUR RELATIONSHIP WITH YOUR GRANDCHILDREN

What kind of a grandparent are you? What kind would you like to be? Do you feel guilty because you cannot comply with what you *think* is expected of you? What do you *feel* is expected of you? What about *your* expectations? Are they unrealistic? Such as expecting your teenage grandchild to spend the entire summer with you when he or she would rather go somewhere else? These are questions you have to ask yourself in order to clear the air of any preconceived ideas and have a good relationship.

How are grandparents who are still very youthful and lead busy lives of their own supposed to act? You don't have to feel old just because you are a grandparent. Elizabeth Taylor and Rhonda Fleming, both grandmothers, are not over the hill yet. Today, grandparents are younger, if not chronologically, certainly in attitude. There are many different types of grandmothers and grandfathers. I was a "baby-sitting grandmother" only once. And I learned something from that experience. My grandson asked me for a glass of freshly squeezed orange juice (he was seven at the time). When he had finished drinking it, he asked for more. "This time, Grandma, I want a big glass." I gave it to him. When he finished the second one, he asked for a third. "You have had enough," I said. "That's it." "Oh, please, Grandma, just one more, only one more, please, please." And so, like most grandmothers, I gave in—after all, I wanted him to love me. No sooner had I given him the orange juice than he said, "Gee, Grandma, you don't know how to say no."

The very same evening I did something similar with my granddaughter. (She was four at the time.) I started to prepare her for bed. She wanted to watch a television program, which was to last a half hour. I gave in. (Oh well, what's a half-hour, I rationalized.) When the program was over, she said, "Please let me watch another program, please, please." So I gave in—how could I say "no?" After all, I wanted her to love me, too. When I finally got her to bed (which was pretty late), and kissed her good night, she looked up at me and said, "You know, Grandma, you don't know how to bring up children." I didn't realize at the time that I was brushing aside their parents' rules. There are times when we feel tempted to do so because we want our grandchildren to love us. But never again did I say "okay" when I wanted to say "no."

If you prefer not to be a baby-sitting grandparent, that's fine. It doesn't mean that you are uncaring and cold. *You have earned the right to peace and quiet now.* It's wonderful to baby-sit if you have the stamina for it, but many grandparents don't. Healthy young children scream, yell, run up and down stairs. After an hour with them you begin to feel like the people who do commercials for headaches. Many of my students have confessed in class that when the Christmas holidays are approaching they can't wait to see their grandchildren. They come down to Florida for ten days or two weeks and the grandparents are absolutely delighted—for one day. After a week, the grandparents are mental and emotional wrecks. They can't cope with bedlam anymore. And they feel guilty.

My students wanted to know if *all* grandparents felt this way. No, all grandparents do not feel this way, but many do. Let your married children and your grandchildren know that you love them, but your nervous system isn't what it used to be, and they will understand. Ellen told her sixteen-year-old granddaughter, emphatically, "I want you home by eleven." "But I'm not a child anymore, Grandma." "I know, that's why I want you home by eleven," Ellen answered. Ellen couldn't handle the responsibility—she was a nervous wreck.

If you are a working grandparent, you may not have the time to devote to your grandchildren. You don't have to feel guilty when you see other grandmothers spending time with their grandchildren. *You can do other things to keep the relationship alive.* Call them on the phone often (if it's long distance it doesn't cost too much after five), just to say, "I called to say I love you." Write to them if they are old enough to read. My daughter used to tell me to print when my grandchildren were first learning to read, and they would write back with X X X X X (kisses) all over the page. The thrill was in receiving a letter addressed to *them*. Send an inexpensive present. It's a waste of money to send expensive presents to very young children, especially if they have a room full of toys. It's the excitement of opening up a package from grandma or grandpa that counts. I used to go to Woolworth's and buy a lot of little things for a few dollars (my daughter gave me that idea). The things were discarded after five minutes, as were any other expensive presents they may have received from the family. Now that they are older, it's different. They know what they want and I prefer to ask them what they would like.

Leave the "parenting" to your married children. Do we have rights as grandparents? Actually, no. You may not approve of the way your married children are bringing up your grandchildren, and suppose you told them so. Where will it get you? Your children have a right to say to you, "Please Mom and Dad, this is *my* child and I'll do what *I* think is best." So where do you stand? Why create dissension? Be the kind of grandparent who is welcomed, not dreaded.

DOES YOUR MARRIAGE NEED REPAIR?

You may recognize that your marriage needs "fixing up," but are unwilling or unable to do anything about it.

Albert and Evelyn have been married thirty years. They have never considered divorce, but they are dissatisfied with their marriage. It became worse when their children left home. Marriage is becoming more and more difficult for them. They still sleep in the same bed, but they live in different worlds. They rarely go anywhere together. They rarely have sex. The "emotional deadness" between them gets across. Finding a new love may be difficult for the person in advanced years, so they stay together. Fixing up the worn-out marriage doesn't occur to them so they do nothing. What a waste of years!

Many unsatisfactory marriages do not break up. Many

couples stay together despite the lack of emotional closeness and live in misery. (Often, however, their behavior toward each other for the outside world is as sweet as maple syrup.) Other couples stay together by avoiding each other as much as possible. I know a retired man in his sixties who became the president of ten civic organizations so that he could be out of the house every day and evening. Saturdays and Sundays "there's always work to be done for the organizations." Why does this couple stay together? Most of the money is in her name. She's willing to give him a divorce but he will have to pay too big a price. He doesn't want to live like a pauper (and she knows it—that's her hold on him), so he sublimates and lives like a king. She gets recognition through him. "Mrs. Smith, you're so lucky to have such a husband. He does so much good. He works so hard for others." Emotionally, she's dead; she believes it's too late to repair her marriage. It's not entirely her fault. *Both* have to work at making marriage stimulating. Sublimation saves him, however. Getting the affection and recognition from the good work he does (and an occasional affair) helps him to survive. Husbands are like wood fires—when unattended, they go out.

Marriage in itself does not make one happy. It's the attitudes we hold regarding marriage that make for marital bliss or marital discord. You can make your fifties or sixties or seventies the most exciting, the most wonderful years of your life. When a man and woman try with all the power that is in them to make their marriage work, the result is ennobling for both.

Incompatibility is a word that is loosely used. After the slightest disagreement, one partner will say, "We are incompatible." What this really means is, right now we don't see eye to eye. When you say you and your spouse are incompatible, you are indicating that there is no hope and that you might as well not put any effort into working out your differences. Your marriage may not be as bad as you think it is. No two people can live in total harmony. One of you would have to be a human vegetable. Little disagreements and different points of view do not destroy a marriage. In fact, they make it more interesting. You are two different personalities. You don't have to agree on everything to be lovable, just disagree with respect for each other. In other words, learn to disagree agreeably, if you want to repair your marriage. I have already talked about giving our children "unconditional love." Husbands and wives need unconditional love, too, for a workable marriage. No spouse can feel secure in marriage when he hears, "As long as you toe the mark, we will get along fine, but if you don't do what I think you *should* do, then I can't love you." There are such marriages (conditional love), but you will find that the one who is "taking it" is always coming down with some kind of psychosomatic illness because of the insecurity involved in conditional love. If you are in an unhappy marriage, don't make a martyr of yourself. Do something to improve the situation.

One of my students told me the following story. A husband got fed up with his wife's nagging, so he simply packed up his personal things and took a small furnished apartment next door so that he could think things through. When they occasionally met in the elevator, they spoke to each other very politely and graciously. Finally one neighbor asked him, "Why did you take an apartment in the same building? Why don't you move away? I used to hear all that nagging and I wondered how you could stand it—she's terrible." "Well, now, I wouldn't say that," the husband said. "You know, she makes a darn good neighbor."

If you must quarrel, try not to be destructive. Don't tear each other down: "You are an idiot." "I don't know why I ever married you." Getting even is childish and destructive. It makes it harder to repair your marriage if you keep on quarreling destructively. If you disagree or do argue, do it constructively. Stick to the issues. Your spouse is not an idiot because he or she disagrees with you. You are expressing *your* point of view. Your spouse has a right to express his or hers. If you see you are getting nowhere, know when to stop. Don't continue the argument—it's like banging your head against the wall. What difference does it make who "wins?" No one really wins in a marital fight.

Some husbands may refuse to listen or even discuss an important problem. They may walk out of the house or go into another room and slam the door. In that case, leave him alone for the time being. When he comes back you might gently say something like this, "Darling, I know you don't like this subject, but we must discuss it and reach a decision. If you persist in running away from it, the problem won't disappear—it will still be here, so whether you enjoy it or not, we must talk it over. I will keep on bringing up the subject if you keep walking away from it because it is *important,* so let's be adult about it." You, as the wife, are asserting yourself, you are not arguing, you are not tearing him down, you are persisting because it is the kind of problem that requires some kind of a decision.

You may be thinking, "Who could live like that? You'd have to be a saint." No, you do not have to be a saint. You just have to train yourself to have emotional control. You are taking constructive action when you assert yourself. It makes you feel better to know that whenever necessary you can and will assert yourself and try to work things out without destroying the marital relationship.

If you are in the habit of reproaching your husband and then one day you decide to make a sexual overture, don't be disappointed if he doesn't respond to you. What he is after is escape from reproach and when he looks at you he doesn't see anything but a symbol of reproach. He knows that your emotional pattern will repeat itself (unless you examine your emotions and make an honest effort to change). Constant reproaching does not repair a marriage. Divorce is not the answer either. The habit of reproach must be removed or you will continue to do the same thing no matter whom you marry. Find new ways to build up the man you've got. Praise him at every opportunity (sincerely). Become a symbol of solace to him. Make it a habit to laugh at his jokes not because they are clever, but because you are. He will then be in a mental and emotional condition to appreciate your sexual overtures.

A few years ago I wrote an article for our local newspaper in Florida entitled, "Cold Cream in Bed Curbs a Husband's Desire." I hope you don't go to bed with cold cream and curlers or toilet paper wrapped around your head (as some women do to keep their hair in place). No husband enjoys making love to cold cream and toilet paper. No matter if you've been married over thirty years, go to bed looking as if you were expecting exciting company. You are—your husband! Husbands are funny creatures. We have to make ourselves exciting to excite them, especially when they are past sixty. Their sexual desire can be kept alive if we incite it. If your husband is retired, he may desire sex at any time, morning, noon, or before dinner. What difference does it make? Remember, he has an unconscious fear of impotency, so don't reject him. This is not to say you must always yield. But if you reject him sexually *too* often, he begins to doubt himself.

Some husbands think that certain foods are sexually stimulating (oysters, seafood, etc.). Because they *believe* it, it works for them. It's not the food—it's their *brain.* That's the greatest aphrodisiac. So feed them anything that they think will make them sexier. When I was married I told my husband that split pea soup was very important in terms of virility. A lot of nonsense—but *I* loved split pea soup and he didn't and I didn't want to cook it just for myself. Suggestion is very powerful; he grew to love split pea soup and I had to make it almost every day and was I sorry I started it.

If you want your husband to eat nutritious food for

health's sake, the power of suggestion works wonders. "This food feeds your sexual glands, dear, try it, it helps to increase sexual vigor." If he *believes* it, it may work. If not, he certainly will be healthier anyway. As it happens, split peas contain a little zinc and zinc *is* important for a man, sexually speaking, so I wasn't exactly lying to my husband. Also, the B vitamins *do* feed the sexual glands, so give your husband plenty of those (and tell him why).

And this, dear husbands, is strictly for you. Don't lash out at your wife with rude impatience if she is not ready to go out at the appointed time. Instead of flaring up and saying a lot of things that create dissension and hostility, it would be wiser if you sat down and calmly read a good book. You will be astonished at the amount of information you can acquire while you are waiting for your wife. Also, it isn't conducive to marital bliss to treat your wife as if she doesn't exist when you are reading a newspaper or watching the football game on television. Look up from your newspaper every once in a while and say something to her. If you are watching the football game, let her know you know she is there. Get up and pat her fanny or throw a kiss or smile at her—do *something* to let her know she's not a piece of furniture. Keep up the romance even when you are watching your favorite game. By your gestures and nonverbal language you are letting her know that you love her and can still think of *her* while watching an exciting game. My, how flattering that is to a woman.

A man does not always understand a woman's hungers. When she seems frustrated, he thinks she wants him to make love to her. She may be hungry for him to notice her new hair style or her new dress or new shoes. (Husbands usually notice them when they get the bills.) She may be hungry for him to verbalize his love for her or to say something about the good dinner she served him. Wives, too, want to be complimented. They, too, need nurturing. A husband who neglects his wife or abuses her verbally cannot expect her to be responsive in lovemaking. Sex does not start in the bedroom.

Jim, an old friend, said to me recently, "I can't understand why Shirley is so indifferent and disagreeable to me. I load her with presents, I try to give her every pleasure. I take her on trips, I take her to places many women would be wild about." When I spoke with his petite, lovely, and nonassertive wife, she said, "Yes, he gives me very expensive presents, but they are always the things that *he* likes, and which do not interest me. And the pleasures are always what he thinks I *ought* to enjoy because *he* enjoys them. I used to pretend at first and act happy about everything because I loved him so much, but I can't keep it up any longer." I asked her if she had told him what *would* give her pleasure. She did, she said, but he thought it was ridiculous and stupid. Since everything had to be *his* way and she couldn't deal with it, the delicious intoxication she once felt when they were together had subsided. I asked Jim, "Would you prefer to give Shirley presents and pleasures which you think she *ought* to like, even though she has shown you that she does not, and lose her love, or would you rather keep her love by giving her what she does desire, regardless of what you think she ought to want?" Of course his answer was the latter.

The following suggestions may help to repair your marriage:

- Respect each other.
- Be tolerant of each other's shortcomings—neither of you is perfect.
- Minimize your spouse's faults and magnify the good points.
- Work on getting rid of destructive habits of responding to each other.
- Try to bring out the best in each other.
- Tell your spouse how you feel about things, but do it gently; don't attack him or her.

- Break up the old patterns of doing things—initiate changes.
- Don't harbor resentment. Talk it out with your spouse or you will communicate your resentment in nonverbal language, which makes for more friction in the relationship.
- Don't be a "house worshipper"; be a husband worshipper. Let your husband enjoy his home; being overly neat and concerned about where he sits or lies down makes him feel like a guest; be more concerned with your husband's comfort.
- After so many years of marriage, it's about time you stopped trying to remodel your spouse. It can't be done that way. Your spouse has to remodel himself by *himself*—that is, if he has the desire to change. No one changes anybody else. People change themselves when they *want* to.
- If your spouse keeps reminding you of past arguments and past issues, say, "Let's forget the past. What can we do *now* to make ours a good relationship? What do we expect of each other now?
- Play problems down—don't exaggerate them.
- Don't embarrass or insult your spouse in front of other people; not only does it make them uncomfortable, but your spouse may explode later and it may escalate into a big fight.
- Both parties have to take steps to repair the marriage. If one spouse just keeps "taking it" and harbors grudges and resentments, the result will be chronic misery and/or psychosomatic symptoms.

- You don't "own" each other; each of you is a free-thinking person in your own right.
- Both spouses have to work at making married life stimulating. Have outside interests; be self-sustaining; a spouse respects a self-sustaining mate.
- Never argue before going to bed; your sleep will be poor. *Always* make up before getting into bed—for health's sake as well as for your marriage.
- Write on a small blackboard, "Making love with you is what sunshine is to a flower"; place it next to the TV (if your TV is in the bedroom).
- Have a discussion as to what has to be changed or adjusted to. It is wiser to save an old marriage than to start a new; a new marriage requires adjustments and changes, too; you have to adjust to a new set of hang-ups, idiosyncrasies, etc. At least you are familiar with the old ones and most likely they are not as bad as you may think.
- Be sure your behavior does not belie your words.
- When your mouth says one thing, such as, "Of course, I love you—need you ask?" and your behavior indicates otherwise, such as lack of consideration, selfishness, the silent treatment, disapproval or irritation, what is your mate to believe? We tend to believe *behavior.*
- Know the difference between an argument and a "discussion."
- Compliment each other at every opportunity.
- Find new ways to praise your spouse.
- Give each other laughter; it's the greatest gift.

- Be refreshing in your appearance.
- Long, flowing nightgowns are sexier for wives past sixty.
- Give each other privacy as well as a little space in the togetherness.
- Try something different; visit places you have never been to; take courses that will stimulate you both—you will have more to talk about.
- Bear in mind that no one "wins" in a marital fight.
- Don't ever stop saying "please" or "thank you."
- Domination in marriage is tyranny. I once heard a speaker say that every married man is dominated by his wife. To demonstrate this, he said to the audience, "Those of you who are dominated by your wives stand on the left side of the room—those who are not stand on the right side." Ninety-nine out of one hundred men stood up and walked to the left side of the room. One man stood on the right side. The speaker said, "What are you doing over there?" "I don't know," the man said. "My wife gave me a push and told me to stand over here."

Is there such a thing as a good, happy marriage? Yes. What makes a happy marriage? Happy people. What makes happy people? A positive approach to life. Therefore, to have a happy marriage, you have to have positive attitudes. Positive attitudes make you more lovable—it's easier to love a person who is positive than one who is negative. So what makes a happy marriage? Two positive-thinking people.

HOW TO HANDLE JEALOUSY

Jealousy, you might say, is like a disease, a painful disease. It wrecks marriages, friendships, business relationships, and most importantly, it consumes the person who has the "disease." Jealousy is an indication of insecurity and inferiority feelings. The jealous person is unsure of himself or herself and feels inadequate. Envy is different from jealousy. It is not as strong an emotion nor is it as painful. When you envy, you would like to have what someone else has—whether it is material things or personality traits or certain talents. Most of us feel a little envious at times—it's quite normal. "I wish I had a new car like John's." "I wish I had a job like his." "I wish I could dance like Lila." "I wish I could be as extroverted as Frank is." "I would love to be able to wear the kind of clothes she wears." There is very little pain involved in envy. The "wishes" are usually dismissed when one recognizes that certain goals are unrealistic. Envy, however, can spur a person on to do things he never dreamed of doing. That's what happened to me.

When my children were adolescents, a good friend of mine, whose children were of the same age, informed me that she had enrolled in college as a freshman and intended to earn a bachelor's degree. She then went on to tell me how exciting it was. I had married at a young age and though I was always taking some kind of course, they were noncredit courses. I wanted to be free in case my children needed me, especially when they went through the children's diseases (measles, scarlet fever, etc.). But now they were adolescents and I had more freedom. I felt a twinge of envy as my friend related the excitement of going to college. I said to myself, "If she can do it, I can do it—I'm just as smart as she is." I called up the college, was informed that there was still time to register, and rushed down to the college full of enthusiasm. I kept thinking, "If she can do it, I can do it," over and over again. That was the beginning of my academic career. I was spurred on because of envy. Ironically, she dropped out—not because she couldn't make it but because she found other ways to occupy her time. I kept going and couldn't stop.

Jealousy is something different. It is a fear that what you have may be taken away from you. There's a lot of insecurity, lack of self-confidence, deep inferiority feelings, and anger involved in jealousy. That's why it's so painful emotionally, for example, when a husband who has a jealous wife speaks to other women at a party or dances with another woman (especially if she's a widow or a divorced woman). The wife becomes tense, anxious, and angry. She thinks, "Maybe she will 'steal' him from me." The wife who has confidence in herself does not suffer when her husband talks with other women at social functions. Her thinking is rational: "I'm glad he's enjoying himself. I'm proud that other women find him stimulating." The jealous wife's thinking is irrational: "Maybe they are making plans to meet somewhere." "Maybe he finds her more attractive and more stimulating." She acts almost paranoid.

This devil of jealousy can make a marriage hell. "Did you have to dance more than one dance with her? Did you have to hold her so tightly?" Sometimes it is normal to feel slightly jealous (it's a matter of *degree*) when a husband goes around kissing and hugging everyone's wife at a party. This behavior is not necessary to have a good time. Deliberate flirting is cruel—it only tortures the jealous spouse. Sometimes men or women past fifty want to convince themselves that they are still attractive to the opposite sex. Don't reproach your spouse, be nice and pleasant and make yourself *more* attractive. It will *pass* if you don't make a big deal of it. Play it down. Husbands who have jealous wives should reassure them constantly that they are loved. Praising the wife, encouraging her to do things which will raise her self-esteem may help, too. The more things one accomplishes, the higher the self-esteem, and the less jealousy. If nothing else works, professional help is needed.

The same applies to a jealous husband. If he acts jealous because his wife looks at another man or talks to other men at social functions, it does not mean that he loves his wife more than a husband who shows no sign of jealousy. The jealous husband feels threatened, afraid that someone may "steal" his wife from him. Many times his fear is unrealistic. He can feel jealous when there's nothing realistically to be threatened about. Jealousy originates in childhood. Overpossessiveness is a childhood trait. If the husband has experienced many failures, his pattern of jealousy becomes worse. If the wife says, "Let's go to the movies tonight—I adore Paul Newman," it triggers his insecurity and inadequacy. If he had more confidence in himself, the remark wouldn't bother him at all. Or if he were just a wee bit jealous (it's the *intensity* of jealousy that has a disastrous effect on marriage), he would possibly be thinking, "Paul Newman is not 'real.' I'm real, I'm here, he's in the movies, he's just a fantasy." A wife may mention to her husband how wonderful his best friend looks since he lost fifteen pounds; the jealous husband feels threatened. "Does she still love me? Maybe I should lose weight, too" (even though he may not be overweight at all). He is always comparing himself with others. If his friend accomplishes something worthwhile, it is painful to him.

Both men and women occasionally feel a *twinge* of jealousy, but the wise spouse is able to control it and does not become unpleasant to live with. When jealousy is not controlled, the other spouse feels possessed, anchored down, stifled. "Where were you all afternoon? What did you do? What took you so long to buy milk?"

Saying to oneself, "Oh God, I wish I could get rid of this jealousy in me," won't help. It reminds me of the two little girls who were late for school. "Let's stop and pray to God to get us there on time," said one. "No," said the other, "let's run with all our might and pray while we are running." Taking constructive action or getting professional help can be very beneficial.

When things are not going well for some people or they are having lots of problems, they are more prone to jealousy attacks. Marge and Ada are best friends. One day, Marge phoned Ada and said, "You must see my new mink coat—come over quickly." Ada rushed over, watched Marge parade all over the living room with her mink coat and then said, "Oh, Marge, your muskrat coat is so . . . I mean, your mink coat is so beautiful." Ada unconsciously would have liked to see Marge in a muskrat coat since that was what *her* husband could afford.

When you recognize that a friend is jealous of you, for whatever reason, cater to your friend's jealousy, if you want the relationship. Your friend can't help getting an attack of jealousy if something good happens to you. Sometimes it may appear to be controlled outwardly, but inside the person is in pain. You may say, "But if my friend really loved me, then he/she would be happy for me." Remember, you are dealing with an insecure person, a person who feels inadequate, which holds him/her back from achieving things or getting the most out of life. Whenever possible, try to build up friends who feel jealous. Look for nice things to say to bolster their self-confidence. Encourage them to do things. The more skills jealous people develop, the more they dilute or minimize their jealousies and inferiorities. Their self-evaluation must be raised. Don't brag or boast about your own achievements—your friend can't take it if the jealousy is too intense. It is difficult to have a satisfying friendship when you know that the other person has a jealous pattern. In the words of George Eliot: "Friendship is the inexpressible comfort of feeling safe with a person, having neither to weigh thoughts nor measure words."

Divorce in the Later Years 6

We all have heard of couples breaking up after twenty or thirty (or more) years of marriage. If a marriage cannot be repaired, it is more beneficial in terms of the mental health of both husband and wife to get a divorce. It doesn't make sense to live in misery. However, as a marriage and family counselor, I encourage couples to iron out their difficulties and at least have a "satisfactory" marriage rather than break up, especially if they are past sixty. But if one or both spouses are too stubborn or rigid to change and make their marriage workable, what else is left but divorce? And divorce is not so terrible. You only have one life and you should get the most out of it.

There are many reasons for divorce in the later years. Since it can be obtained more easily now, people are reevaluating their marriages. Wives are initiating divorce as well as husbands. Some women feel that if they get a divorce, there's always the possibility of finding someone else or creating a new life and finding some fulfillment. When their children were very young they didn't have the nerve to do it. Now that the children are grown and out of the house, a wife or husband may feel that he or she wants another chance at happiness. One partner may have outgrown the other and derives no satisfaction from the marriage. Another reason may be that when a wife goes back to work because she's tired of being in the kitchen, the husband may resent it. Dinners are fast or they may have to eat out more often, whereas before the wife had time to make his favorite dishes and perhaps cater more to him. Or a husband may have too much time on his hands when his wife resumes her career and will find someone else to fulfill his needs. Some husbands need to convince themselves that they can still "make it" with another woman—they feel that making love to the same woman for thirty years doesn't prove anything, so they throw themselves into promiscuity to test their masculinity.

Even when divorce is feasible it is not the whole answer for certain people. When you get out of a bad marriage you may feel relieved for a while. But if you are not prepared to face life alone mentally and emotionally (and financially); if you cannot face "aloneness" or loneliness and you become even more insecure or more depressed, what have you gained? *Before* you make the break, prepare yourself psychologically. Some women and men prepare themselves before the actual legal divorce takes place (while they are in a state of emotional divorce) by finding someone else. They suffer less. They are not alone after the divorce. If you cannot do this, then prepare yourself mentally by imagining yourself in your mind's eye dining alone, being alone night after night, doing everything alone. Don't imagine yourself doing any of these things with friends—you are *alone.* Can you take it? Does it frighten you? If so, you are not ready. You need to work on yourself. Living alone is really not so bad. You can accustom yourself to anything if your attitude is good. You will experience a power you never knew you had. If you can handle it, go ahead and get a divorce.

A woman of sixty said to me, "I would rather have my lousy marriage than no marriage. I can't stand being alone and I'm afraid I won't meet another man at my age to remarry. I've grown accustomed to my fate." No one has to resign himself to unhappiness. There's always a way out, *if one wants* to pay the price. In her case, the possibility of loneliness is the price. And even then she may not have to continue paying the price if she learns how to deal with loneliness.

How you perceive your divorce will determine how quickly you will recover from your loss (even though you are not a widow, a loss is still a loss). The way you are going to feel depends on the way you think. If you tell yourself, "This is terrible. How could it happen to me? How could he leave me after so many years of marriage? Life is not worth living anymore," you will sink; you will destroy yourself. What happens to you after the divorce depends on *you*. It is not the end of the world. There is always the possibility that life can become better and more meaningful for you.

You may have a need to "talk" while you are going through the divorce or afterward. Get it out of your system —talk to someone you trust. But don't keep rehashing the past. It's over—finished. Tell yourself he or she no longer exists for you.

If Only . . .

If you find yourself thinking, "If only I had been nicer . . . if only I had given him more sex . . . if only I had made myself more attractive . . . if only I hadn't insisted on winning every argument . . ." The "if onlys' " are endless. Learn from your past mistakes so that you don't repeat the same behavior should you find someone else, and stop torturing yourself. You are only defeating yourself. You cannot undo what you have already done. Go forward now with more experience as to what to do and what not to do in another relationship.

What Do I Do Now?

Start living in the present. Stop talking about your misfortune and start thinking about a new life. Watch your health more closely. You don't want to get any stress-related diseases, which sometimes occur when one cannot cope with change. Change may be frightening, but you will survive. Pick yourself up and begin a new life no matter how painful it is for you. You must literally force yourself to do things and move ahead despite the emotional pain. Tell yourself, "I can do it in spite of this fear, in spite of this emotional discomfort." Your attitude is most important. You must believe that you can have a fresh start, that life has a lot to offer. *You* have to assume the responsibility for creating your own happiness. No one will come knocking at your door. It doesn't matter how old you are, or whether you were thrown over for a younger person or a more fascinating person. The fact is that it's over and finished. It will not change things for you if you remain floored by your divorce. Remember, it's no disgrace to fall in the mud—the disgrace is to lie there.

Expand your social life. Let people know that you are available. However, don't depend on married friends for companionship. Seek out other singles. Learning to cope with newly found freedom can be tough at times, but you will manage it. Use your grit. Get off your fanny and look for the circumstances you want. Go to places where you will meet the kind of people you may have something in common with. If you can afford it, take trips. I know of many cases where women met men away from their home town and later on communicated by letter and phone and eventually got married. Don't feel embarrassed going places alone. You are much better off even if it costs more to travel as a single. If you are alone, you don't have to be concerned about your traveling companion should you meet someone who wants to be with you and you with him. Don't fear rejection. Do things you never did before. Take a "so what?" attitude toward rejection. Teach yourself to become immune to rejection. Don't be shocked or disappointed if your married friends stop inviting you to their homes. They may feel uncomfortable with you as an "extra woman." Women who are insecure in their own marriage may feel too threatened to have you around. Do anything that will give you a lift psychologically and spiritually. Go to a good hairdresser; change your hairstyle or color; buy new clothes. Become a new you. Don't turn to food for comfort. Find other outlets. If you are overweight, join a health club. Read the section on "How to Lose Weight Easily" again. You can also look for some kind of work which will satisfy you and at the same time present opportunities to meet people.

Try to meet men even though you may not wish to remarry. Start dating. Even if the man isn't exactly what you are looking for, but is pleasant, go out anyway just for *experience*. If you are past fifty, perhaps you haven't dated for twenty or thirty years. Dating will help you feel more comfortable when you finally do meet a man you really like.

I don't think it is necessary to rush into sexual intimacy after a divorce to restore a loss of self-esteem. It doesn't prove anything. To some men, sex is like shaking hands. Other men are only interested in one-night stands. I'm talking about men past sixty, too. If you want to fool yourself and think you are "wanted" forever, get rid of the delusion. The man who really "wants" you will not rush you into bed the first night. You don't have to use sex as a means to gain self-confidence. If you don't want to go to bed with a man, you can afford emotionally to say, "No." If he doesn't call again, so what? Is that going to lower your self-esteem more? Is that all you think of yourself? There's a wonderful human being attached to your vagina. If he hasn't discovered that you are a "person," not just a vagina, that's *his* loss. If you meet someone you really like and he looks upon you as a human being *first*—someone to talk to and laugh with, someone to go places with—the sexual intimacy will bring you closer together. *Now* you are a woman who is *really* wanted.

Susan, fifty-nine, divorced about four months, and

twenty-five pounds overweight, met a widower of sixty-four (also somewhat overweight) at a social function. They hit it off beautifully. After a few weeks, he suggested going to bed. He didn't want to rush her, he said, but he felt that since neither of them was dating anyone else, he would like a closer relationship. Susan avoided sexual intimacy as long as she could because she was ashamed of her body. She had a lovely face and knew how to camouflage her excess weight with the proper clothes. Finally, the man said to her, "I guess you don't feel the same way about me. I was hoping our relationship would lead to something more than just friendship. Perhaps we should call it quits." She started to cry and explained to him that she hadn't been to bed with any man other than her husband in thirty-nine years (she was married at twenty). "So what's the problem?" he asked. "I'm overweight," she said, "You can't see it because of the undergarments and clothes I wear." He started to laugh, "I thought it was something serious. Look at me. I'm overweight, too. I have a pot belly, but I'm not ashamed. We will both diet together, but let's have fun while we are dieting. Maybe we will lose weight faster—we won't be eating so much." They are still together and both have lost weight. Susan told me they are planning to get married and that she never dreamed that kind of "fun" could take the place of food for her. Being involved in a personal relationship that is gratifying makes one realize there is more to life than just eating.

REMARRIAGE

Milton and Sandra had been married just two weeks when he was going through a batch of mail that had arrived that morning. "Honey, aren't these bills for the clothes you bought *before* we were married?" Milton asked indignantly. "Yes, darling, you're not upset about it, are you?" "Well, don't you think it's unfair to ask a fish to pay for the bait he was caught with?" Milton and Sandra married for the wrong reasons. He thought she had money and she thought he had money. Their marriage didn't last long. Had they been honest with each other and discussed what they expected of each other, they could have avoided another divorce.

A widower who had married again told me, "I wasn't any different in my first marriage, but my second wife wouldn't put up with my nonsense so she divorced me. My first wife got used to my nonsense." When people are unwilling to change they marry, divorce, marry, divorce, again and again. A new marriage can be wonderful if a person is willing to change certain behavior patterns.

A twice-married man in his sixties told me, "I learned a lot from my first marriage. I pay more attention to my second wife. I don't take her for granted. I'm far more considerate than I was in my first marriage. I'm happier in my second marriage. I changed in many ways. I'm a good listener, now. I allow my second wife to express herself, to ventilate any problems. We have a great marriage."

Grown children may cause problems for parents wishing to remarry, especially if the parents are very well off financially. The children may be looking forward to inheriting the money. I know a wealthy widower in his late sixties who is very much in love with a widow who was left very little money. When he told his three grown sons that he was planning to marry her, they said to him, "Why do you want to get married? Live with her. Everybody is doing it. You don't have to be married today—be modern. Besides, you're ten years older than she. How do you know she's not after your money?" It so happens that this fine lady is very much in love with him and he knows it. The father knew his sons were more concerned about his money than his happiness.

He was very direct, "Listen, sons, don't worry about your share of the money. I'm still alive and I intend to live it up while I can. I would not feel comfortable 'living' with her—besides, I want her to be my *wife.*" He got married and his sons didn't speak to him for months. The wife brought them together at a party she gave. When they saw how happy he was and how she took care of him and catered to him, they felt ashamed and apologized to their father.

Sometimes the children's feelings have nothing to do with money. Grown children may feel resentful of a new woman in their father's life (or a new man in their mother's life). This has to do with possessiveness. "How could Dad (or Mom) do this—sleep with another person in the same bed my own mother (or father) slept in?" On the other hand, most grown children welcome the remarriage. They realize that there is a continued need for companionship and they feel relieved knowing that the widowed or divorced parent has found someone.

If your grown children object to your remarrying, have a talk with them. Ask them why they feel as they do. They may have an unrealistic point of view. In any event, do what you think is right for *you.* Just as they lead their own lives without interference from you, you have to do what is best for you.

You are more experienced at marriage now. You know what you did not want or like in your first marriage, so you will carefully choose what you *do* want in your next marriage. If you don't know what you are looking for, how can you find it? Are you looking for a man who does not make too many demands on you? Let's say you don't like having to get up at 7 A.M. to make breakfast for your new husband. At this stage in life you want to sleep later—you want to take it easy. So don't marry a man who *expects* you to rise at 7 A.M. because he does to make breakfast for him. If you can reach a compromise, "I'll make lunch for you and dinner for you, but I want to feel that I can sleep as late as I want," then you may not have a problem. It's wiser to discuss what is expected of each other. You avoid a great deal of conflict, guilt feelings, and disharmony.

Do you want a man who has a sense of humor? If he doesn't have a sense of humor *before* marriage, he won't have one after marriage. That's his personality. Either take him as he is or run the other way. There are pluses and minuses in every relationship—don't look for a *perfect* mate. If there are more pluses, concentrate on those and ignore the minuses. When you spend a lot of time with someone before marriage, personality traits come out sooner or later. Observe them. Is he even-tempered? How does he treat sales clerks and other people? Is he considerate? Thoughtful?

If your future mate knows he has a temper, he may control it very well before marriage, but *after* marriage, he may say, "I can't control my temper—that's the way I am." How come he could control it *before* marriage? Because he wanted to.

Don't delude yourself. There are new adjustments to make in a new marriage, a whole new set of neuroses to adapt to. But if you are not looking for a perfect mate, you can still have a good marriage. *Everyone* is a little neurotic at times. As one of my professors at college said once, "It's abnormal to be one hundred percent normal."

Bear in mind that no one acts in a rational manner *all* the time. If your new mate acts rationally most of the time —wonderful. You can stand a bit of irrationality—ignore it —don't respond to it. Keep your cool, refuse to argue. When one is irrational he is acting like a child. Are you going to argue with a child? Can you reason with a child? Wait until your mate has cooled down—then, calmly say, "I didn't like your behavior the other day. I don't like to be shouted at. If you want to discuss something with me, I'm willing to listen. When you shout, rant, and rave, I close my ears." I'm not saying you are going to change him, but at least he will know how you feel and that a *tantrum* doesn't pay off. When you don't yield to an adult tantrum many times the person changes. He begins to realize he's getting nowhere.

It is difficult to estimate the degree of success achieved in remarriages. We can only assume that a good remarriage is one in which the husband and wife have few complaints.

Generally, people try harder the second time. Their attitude in most cases is, "We want to prove we can make it work." Even though some remarriages do not make it, the agony and the ecstasy of the marital relationship still make taking the emotional trip to the altar again (and again and again) worthwhile. That is what keeps one young. The excitement of a new love relationship should not be underestimated.

How to Handle Loneliness
7

Some people equate aloneness with loneliness. Loneliness and being alone are not the same. Many people live alone, but are not lonely. They like their own company. They can be alone with their thoughts. People who feel this way usually lead full lives, have good relationships with other people, and are glad to have some solitude. To be able to be alone indicates strength and emotional maturity. Chronic loneliness indicates weakness and immaturity. While it is true that everyone feels lonely sometimes, there are degrees of loneliness. Some experience it occasionally and others are always lonely.

Chronic loneliness is a state of mind—a neurotic state of mind. A lonely person is usually one who is a "leaner." He leans on others for emotional comfort. He needs someone all the time to help him face the world. When he can't find anyone who will give him the support he needs, loneliness becomes torture for him and may lead to depression or abuse of alcohol. Lonely people demand too much; as a result, people avoid them and their loneliness is reinforced. People who lack self-confidence, have many inferiority feelings, and do not relate well to others generally suffer the most from loneliness. They usually deal with their loneliness destructively in overeating, overindulging in alcohol, promiscuity, and psychosomatic illnesses.

Solitude is healthy. We all need to be alone at times to think, to relax, to do what we want to do. Some newly divorced or widowed people are able to handle loneliness very well. They simply ignore it and go on living. They feel rather comfortable, a little lonely, but not sad or depressed. (Remember, people who are married can be lonely, too. They lack a meaningful relationship in spite of the fact that they are husband and wife. They may have married for the wrong reasons, one of which may have been to escape loneliness.)

Some widowed and divorced people, who have adjusted to their single state do not wish to marry again. They enjoy their freedom. They lead wonderful, useful, full lives. They like to be alone part of the time and seek company when they choose to. Some people in the later years no longer want a man-woman relationship. They are not comfortable with the demands of intimacy. They prefer sleeping alone. If these people get divorced, they do not experience the pain or loneliness others do. In fact, they feel more comfortable.

However, loneliness has no age and will never be wiped out. Some people are not self-sufficient. They have been overprotected, first by their parents and then by their spouses, and when they find themselves alone with no emotional supports they fall apart. Many look for excuses to avoid the possibility of frustration, disappointment, or rejection and so they do nothing but bemoan their fate. They pursue no new interests, they seek no new friendships, they live in quiet desperation. Handling loneliness requires *action*. If you are lonely you have a choice—you can remain lonely and live a miserable life or you can start doing something about it right now. It's your choice.

COMBATING LONELINESS

- Identify the cause of your loneliness first. Does your loneliness stem from lack of self-confidence and inferiority feelings? Are you lonely because you don't know where to go to meet people? Are you lonely because you feel no one can take the place of your deceased spouse? Are you lonely because of your lifestyle? Are you lonely because you moved to another state and can't make "real" friends? Understanding the *cause* of your loneliness is very helpful in terms of taking the right kind of action to alleviate the pain.
- Cultivate a positive philosophy of life.
- Cultivate new interests.
- Don't sit back and wait for people to come to you. Call up someone and ask him to go to the movies with you, or have dinner with you. If the person is busy, go alone.
- Smile even if you are hurting emotionally. In the words of William James, the father of American psychology, "We do not smile because we are happy; we are happy because we smile." So smile and the hurt of loneliness will gradually diminish.
- Make it known that you want to meet people.
- Don't mess up (unconsciously) the possibility of establishing a new relationship because of your inferiorities and fears. Take a chance. What have you got to lose? Ask yourself, "What is the worst thing that could happen? Rejection?" Then answer yourself, "I could cope with that—I can learn to take it."
- A new man or woman is not the *only* source

of happiness, so find new ways to enjoy life. Many of my students are in their seventies (widows, widowers, divorced)—they are active, vital, enthusiastic, busy every day, and practically every evening, with courses in adult education, charity work, dancing lessons, social functions. It is either develop new resources and new interests or perish.

- Do not indulge in self-pity. Make up your mind you have no one to lean on but yourself. The more self-sufficient you become the more you will be admired and the more people will gravitate toward you.
- Change your self-image. See yourself in your mind's eye as a fun-loving, outgoing, confident person. Do not visualize yourself as shy, timid, awkward. As you act, so you will become.
- If you are invited to dinner at someone's home, don't say, "Are you sure you want me to come? You're having all couples." There's only one answer if you want to go, "Thank you, I'd love to come."
- Let others know about your hobbies and interests. You may discover others who have the same interests.
- Entertain even if you have a small apartment. Invite acquaintances—they may invite you back and you will meet others through them.
- The person sitting next to you at a lecture or in church or synagogue may be lonely, too, and will welcome your friendliness. Many of my female students past fifty told me that they have met widowers or divorced men in

a synagogue or church and developed beautiful relationships.
- Try art galleries if that's your interest.
- Some people past fifty or sixty find singles' clubs comfortable. Others find them uncomfortable. Do what makes *you* feel good.
- Even if you don't need the money, find an interesting job just for human contact.
- Go *alone* to parties. When you are ready to leave, you can just pick yourself up and go without feeling guilty because the person you brought wants to stay.
- If loneliness takes hold of you in the midst of a large party where everyone is having fun, laughing and dancing, don't panic. Each of us has had this feeling at one time or another. Sure, it's wonderful to have affection, but if at the present time, there's no one in your life that nourishes you, so what? You can still nourish yourself. Begin to love *you*. The lonely person doesn't like himself; otherwise he wouldn't be lonely. He can't stand his own company. If you can't stand yourself, how do you expect someone else to like you?
- Look around you. There are millions of people who are either widowed or divorced. Try to emulate the ones who are enjoying their lives.
- Don't react to tactless remarks from married people such as, "It must be awful to be single again at your age."
- Always have new books and magazines around to encourage you, stimulate you, or just amuse you.

- Try different things. How do you know, for example, that you can't paint or knit or write, unless you try?
- Go to the best restaurant in town alone. The maitre d' usually asks, "Are you alone?" as if it's very unusual to be alone. Be confident. "Yes, I'm alone and I would like a good table."
- Don't be afraid to approach other people who are alone. One of my students, a widow of sixty, learned to assert herself in this way. She noticed a woman sitting alone at a nearby table. She walked over to her (which at one time she was never able to do), and asked if she could join her. They discovered they had a lot in common. She made a friend that evening. She came to class the next evening bursting with pride. "I did something I never did before—I felt wonderful," she said.
- If you travel alone, you go when it suits you and you return when it suits you. You are also free for romance if it presents itself. Most likely, you will meet other single people, too.
- Go to department stores and the supermarket *alone*. I have met some very nice men just standing up in the check-out line. It seems so natural to talk. I once said to a man, "Oh, I see you like lamb chops, too." "Yes, I usually freeze the rest," he said. "It hardly seems worth the mess cooking for one, but I love to eat and I get tired of eating out." He was letting me know he was single. "I understand how you feel," I said. "I have the same problem." I was letting him know I was single.
- Try to be with people who have a way of bringing out the best in you.

- Do not believe that having an affair is the *only* antidote to loneliness. However, if you decide that you want an affair, don't make it more than it is. Your only purpose is enjoyment—going places, doing things together. You do not have to play the role of housekeeper, laundress, and cook. Preserve your privacy (i.e. don't hand out the key to your apartment). Living alone, you have the advantage of always looking your best when you see your date. If your affair turns into a deep love and you do begin to think of marriage, you might as well bring up the subject. If your partner backs away, you know where you stand. You have a choice—you can either continue the affair or end it. But you shouldn't be afraid to bring up the subject of marriage—not to know where you stand will only make you tense and anxious. If your goal has changed to marriage, having an affair with a man or woman who is opposed to it (or can't get married for some reason) is like drinking soup with a fork—you only get the exercise.
- It doesn't matter if you are fifty, sixty, seventy, or beyond, you are entitled to enjoy your life. Living alone can be very enjoyable or miserable. Which depends entirely on your attitude.

THE SINGLE LIFE AFTER FIFTY

When you think about romance do you have images in your mind of young people kissing and caressing each other? Most likely you do. Do you also have images of older men and women in their sixties and seventies making love? Probably not. Why not? Sex is not limited to the young. Some grown children may think it's outrageous for a divorced or widowed parent to have a sexual relationship. Yet, it's okay to give an eighteen-year-old granddaughter the pill. At least you don't have to worry about pregnancy (unless you are a very young grandmother). We can, at last, relax. I haven't come across any law that says single grandmothers have to abstain from sex.

Love is wonderful at any age. Older men and women have a right to the comfort of a good, loving sexual relationship. If you are in a love relationship now or ever have been, you know the feeling. It cannot be described in words other than to say you feel like a significant human being. However, you can feel like a worthwhile person even if you are not in a love relationship. The absence of a love relationship causes unhappiness and depression only if a person *believes* that he can't be happy without it. Life without love is still worth living.

At this stage in life, sex may be secondary—it's no longer on the top of the list for some people in advanced years. Affairs often become more psychological than physical. One of my students, a tall, slender woman of seventy, remarried for the third time. Her new husband was seventy-four. Six months later she wanted a divorce. When I asked her why, she said, "I didn't get married to wash his laundry—I got married because I wanted a bed partner. He's not good enough sexually for me anymore." On the other hand, another student who is sixty-seven made a statement in class that at sixty and beyond nobody had sexual desires anymore. Practically everyone in the class shouted at her, "Speak for yourself!" This woman apparently does not (and perhaps never did) enjoy sex and has sexual guilt feelings. "You're supposed to forget that 'foolishness' at this age," she said. That's *her* opinion.

Some men may feel that a widow or divorcee is not really

living if she doesn't have frequent sex. My female students tell me that they often hear from men, "What have you got to lose? Live! Have fun. Life is short, etc." They feel bad. They tell me, "I don't want to be just a sex object" (the cry of most women). I tell them they don't have to feel bad; they should feel flattered. They can always decline the invitation to bed. The important thing is to be honest. If they don't want to have sex, they have no obligation to the man. Rhoda, a divorcee of fifty-eight, learned to say "no" gracefully. "I'm not ready to go to bed. I don't want to become involved." "Who's asking you to become involved with me?" the man argued. "I'm only asking you to have some fun." If a man really likes a woman, the relationship will develop regardless of sex, and if sexual relations do take place eventually, they will be more fulfilling. One of my older male students (seventy-two) has already learned, he said, that pure physical sex is empty—it means nothing unless there is an emotional feeling between the partners. He doesn't have the energy anymore to go from bed to bed.

Jenny, a widow of fifty-five, let a man persuade her that the world had changed and that she would be better off socially if she had a few affairs—she wouldn't be so lonely. He wanted first crack at it, of course, and so she went to bed with him. She felt terrible afterwards. It had no meaning—she had no real feeling for the man, nor did he for her. Her friends were so casual about sex she thought she could emulate them. She discovered it made her feel worse. What's good for one is not always good for another. Sex used as an antidote to loneliness or boredom or as a payment of gratitude is not gratifying emotionally or sexually.

Being single again in your fifties or sixties or beyond, you may begin to wonder if you will ever love again or be loved again by someone of the opposite sex. Many people feel this way. It's not uncommon. The single life past fifty is not easy for some women. They grasp at straws. The good judgment they once had seems to vanish because they want to love and be loved so badly. As a result, they become involved with the wrong partners for them and when the man stops calling for no apparent reason, they feel terribly inadequate: "I can't hold a man." If the relationship with the wrong partner does continue, the woman takes a psychic beating.

Julia became involved with a man who was incapable of satisfying any woman's emotional needs. Julia gave of herself and her emotions; she did things for him, cooked dinners for him, and was always catering to him. He just took. He *expected* these things from her but he gave nothing of himself. She began to feel that she was being used for sexual satisfaction and for the wonderful dinners she cooked. She realized that he had no concern for her as a person. He wasn't interested in any of her personal problems or anything else that was meaningful to her. Resentment and hostility generated in her and manifested themselves in many ways. One day he said to her, "I don't know what's come over you. You're different; you're not the same woman. You're difficult to get along with now." Afraid to lose him completely, she again tried to be what he wanted her to be, but the hostility was still there. She could not say to him, "I feel resentment because you take no interest in me as a person. You are not interested in *my* problems. You are only interested in what I can do for you." She couldn't say it because deep down inside her she knew that his "proclaimed" love was nothing more than pseudo-love and she couldn't face it. "It's better than nothing," she kept telling herself. "I'm getting older. I may not meet anyone else." That was just a rationalization. The real issue was that the man fulfilled a desperate need in her brought about by the fear of loneliness. Pseudo-love or not, she was addicted. She was hooked on love as if she were hooked on drugs. She continued the relationship until she began to suffer from psychosomatic illnesses caused by her fears and repressed emotions. That's when she came to me for counseling. Ironically, she used sex to express hatred. She became very aggressive and tore at him sexually. She bit him, scratched him during sex and he thought she had become more passionate. She had—sadistically so. "You used to be so tender and gentle," he said. "You're a ball of fire now. You hurt me—look at the marks I have on my bare skin." Her hate was masquerading as passion. She learned that her desperate need to love and be loved only made her less desirable to men. When she learned how to deal with loneliness, and relax when she was out with a man, she finally found someone who was worthy of her love.

Don't waste time at this stage in life. If you recognize that your partner is not for you, sever the relationship quickly. Find someone who will satisfy *your* emotional needs, too. However, some people no longer want an intimate relationship. They are involved in good causes, work that satisfies them, they have their children and grandchildren, they are happy without a partner. The older woman or man who decides to live in celibacy is just as normal as the person who still enjoys sex.

There are other problems that single people past fifty encounter. A woman may not want to give up her alimony check, so she stays single. A man may be interested more in a woman's bank account than in her—especially if she is a widow. I have had men ask me what kind of paintings I own, what kind of a car I drive, whether I work because I *have* to or because I have nothing else to do, how much rent I pay, and so on. Men come to Florida from all over the country on a pension and figure they have it made with at least twenty-five widows to one man. Now, I'm not saying that all older men are like that—some are darn nice and don't want or need a woman's money. I'm just amused by the other kind. I have found that when widowers or divorced men can afford a maid and/or cook or live in an apartment hotel with maid service and a restaurant in the building, they are not in a rush to get married again. In fact, they often prefer not to remarry. Date? Yes. Companionship? Yes. Sex? Yes. But marriage, no.

The men who cannot afford maids and cooks seem to be more anxious to get married. They have their complaints. "Women don't want to cook anymore. They just want to have a good time." Many of my older male students have told me this. They may be looking in the wrong places. There are women who love to cook and want a home life with a man.

One of the problems single women face is how to get a man to take you out without having to "give in." Penny, fifty, divorced about two years, solved the problem this way: A man she knew slightly called her one evening and said, "Would you like to have D and B Saturday evening?" "Oh, I'd love to," she said, not really understanding what D and B meant. They had dinner at a lovely place and afterward he said to her, "Now where shall we go for B—your place or mine?" She finally got the message. She then explained to him that she didn't know that D and B meant Dinner and Bed. She thought it was some kind of a drink. "Oh, come now," he said, "don't kid me—you've been around." "Well," she said, "I'm really not ready for you tonight, but when I am you will be number one on my list." He kept calling her for weeks, she told me, hoping he would be number one. In the meantime, a friendship developed and he discovered that she had some wonderful qualities and that he enjoyed her company. The point here is: in similar situations when she acted offended and told the men off, she lost them. But when she changed her attitude and could laugh about it and feel flattered instead of offended, she had ten men waiting to be number one. She is still using this line and it still works. All is fair in dating and war. She's not deceiving any man. If a man wants to wait to be number one, that's *his* business. She's not promising anything—she's only saying, "When I'm ready . . ."

Many of my female students have asked me how I handle

the "seduction" situation since I, too, am single. I tell them this story: A friend had arranged a blind date for me with a man of sixty. When he called he sounded very nice and so I went out with him. He suggested a romantic place to dine and dance. It was fine with me. As we were dancing, he bragged about his sexual escapades, which turned me off. But I enjoy dancing and so the evening was not entirely a flop for me. At the end of the evening, I thanked him, and as he walked me to my door, he asked to come in for a nightcap. Getting the message from the gleam in his eyes, I said, "I'm afraid that my awareness of your proclivities in the esoteric aspects of sexual behavior precludes you from such erotic confrontation." "I don't get it," he said. "Exactly," I responded.

IF YOU ARE LIVING AWAY FROM YOUR CHILDREN AND FAMILY

If you found it necessary to move to another state, for the warmer climate because of ill health, or for whatever reason, loneliness need not be a problem. The first few months away from your family, your lonely feelings may be at their strongest, but as time goes on you will accustom yourself to the change.

Don't depend on your children for too many visits—it's a burden on them. When you move away from your family and children you have to make a new life for yourself. Your children will love you more and respect you more knowing that you are happy and creating a new life. You will relieve them of guilt feelings.

Don't phone them every day. Don't make them feel guilty for not calling or visiting as often as you would like. They are busy people. It takes courage to change your lifestyle and go forward to a new one. You already took the first step when you moved. Though you may still experience a sense of longing—a yearning to be with them—you will eventually adapt yourself to your new circumstances.

Begin to do things to assuage your loneliness. Look to comfort others who are worse off than you are. Seek activities that interest you. Most importantly, *keep busy*.

FEAR OF BECOMING ILL WHEN LIVING ALONE

First of all, don't dwell on illness. When people think about illness constantly they get sick. Think through once and for all what you will do in the event that you do become ill and then stop dwelling on it.

Fear of illness may have other emotional components. A person may unconsciously want someone to take care of him. Life may be too rough for the person, so he concentrates on illness, which is an escape from his problems. Think about your problems instead and decide what to do about them. If you can't resolve certain problems, acceptance of them and a change of attitude is a solution, too.

The following guidelines may help to allay your fear of illness:

- Paste the telephone number of the Rescue Squad and the local police station on your telephone.
- Paste the phone number of a friend or neighbor on your night table. When one is frightened, one has a tendency to block out telephone numbers.

- Become friendly with more than one neighbor and explain to them that in the event they needed you, you would do the same for them. Paste their numbers on your night table, too (near your bed).
- You can always dial the operator and ask for help if you can't get a neighbor or you can't dial the complete number of the Rescue Squad.

How to Improve Your Sex Life

8

It's not difficult to be a good lover—one who is skilled in "making love." Anyone who wants to can master the contents of a book on sexual techniques. Nothing else matters to the person if he wants to become a sexual athlete. It is the greatest and most thrilling game in the world to some people. "Every woman can be had," a divorced man in his late fifties told me. "You just have to know how to go about it." "Every man can be turned on if you have the right technique," a newly divorced woman of fifty-one indicated in one of my classes. One just has to be an "artist" in making love—the quintessence of the sexual revolution. Some people develop a sexual technique as highly specialized as the technique of a surgeon. Are they happy? Yes, but their happiness many times is short-lived.

What most women are hungry for is a man who has "principle" underlying his expertness—a man who stands for something outside his sexual virtuosity; a man who is kind, compassionate, and capable of loving.

To some men, sex is a physiological exercise that has no more emotional content than evacuation of bowels and bladder. Consequently, no sexual intimacy can relieve their sense of isolation and loneliness. Many unmarried (and married) men in their late fifties and sixties who are still searching for sexual conquests in their attempt to be "every inch a man" are confused about true virility. It is not necessary to have "proof" of one's virility to be virile. This is why some men often "kiss and tell"—they brag about their exploits to other men and women because they have to reassure themselves constantly that they are virile. If a man has unconscious self-doubts in terms of his virility, making love to the same woman all the time will not relieve his anxiety. To be successful with one woman is not enough—he is compelled to find out whether he can succeed with others. Because of his neurotic need for "applause" in the bedroom he is driven into promiscuity.

Promiscuity may help a man temporarily to forget his conflicts, his fears, his inadequacies (just as alcohol does), but sooner or later he has to face himself. He cannot be a sexual athlete forever. Edward, sixty, divorced for ten years, confessed with tears in his eyes that the Don Juan route had finally gotten to him. "To make love without love is so empty," he said. "Most times I couldn't wait to get away from the woman afterward. Sometimes the pleasure, the triumph would last two nights, three nights, a week, and then, emptiness again. I felt compelled to go on to another woman." Now Edward was nervous and depressed. The whole sexual game had lost its flavor. He was getting older and the fear of failing in the bedroom had gotten to him. He was beginning to feel that his repertoire of sexual virtuosity was coming to an end. He realized his inability to love and hold the love of a woman and he was afraid of facing old age alone.

There are many men who become bored with a woman after sexual relations and can't wait until they can get away. But when a man has a genuine feeling for the woman, when he really loves, even after he is sexually satisfied he still desires her because love cannot be satisfied once and for all.

Sex can be strangely beautiful, sex can be disgusting; sex can be lustful, sex can be holy; sex can be the profound mystery of nothing, sex can be the profound mystery of everything; sex can be a curse, sex can be a blessing; sex can be madness, sex can be a rejuvenation; sex can be the fulfillment of a couple's love, sex can be the expression of a neurosis.

SEX IS NOT ENOUGH

Once upon a time sex was not considered a "problem." It was the natural course of events, and all in the day's work. But that was in the "good old days" when a man was supreme master of his wife simply because he was a man, a superior being, and his woman was something he owned. Woman submitted.

But now all has changed. Woman has asserted her independence; she has become an individual. She has strong likes and dislikes; tastes and aspirations beyond the mere ministering to her man and so she cannot be expected to be quite so "tranquil" a sexual companion.

No wonder sex has become a problem. So much "sensational" and misleading material has been written on the subject that many people have developed *new* problems regarding their sexual lives. Technique is stressed so much that people have developed anxieties in terms of sexual performance. The popular sex books seem to be saying: Perfect your sexual technique and you will have a good relationship, a good marriage; everything will be wonderful. What nonsense!

When sexual satisfaction is dependent on technique alone rather than on emotional feeling between the two partners, full gratification is rarely achieved. Sexual technique can be helpful, but it is the *relationship* that determines the quality of the sex rather than the techniques. Women are being bombarded with advice on how to develop a "sexual personality" and encouraged to devote a great deal of their time to the erotic life. To become obsessed with developing a "sexual personality" in terms of how good you are in bed, or how many orgasms you can have in one night or help your partner to have, may lead to a neurosis. We all know that sex is here to stay and each of us must come to terms with our own sexual impulses. Very few people have exactly the same sexual tastes when they get together. Sex is not a perfect game—neither are human beings perfect.

One of my students, a married woman of fifty-nine, indicated to me privately that her husband has gone haywire since reading all the popular sex books. He has become so demanding she doesn't know what to do. Another student, Bob, a handsome man of sixty-one, said that his wife, who is five years younger than he (she was not in class that day), has recently been reading so much on the subject of sex that he has developed problems he never had before regarding their sexual life. He has become obsessed with "technique," he said, and no longer finds sex relaxing.

Sex is not a test you must struggle not to flunk. It is not crucial to your existence. Young, middle-aged, older people are all seeking to solve the most baffling problem of life—freedom of sex in a setting of dignity.

A man wants a lovable sweetheart or wife who combines within her own personality the dignity of the madonna with the free vivacity of the whore. We all have heard the slogan, "A cook in the kitchen, a lady in the living room, and a whore in the bedroom." Great! If one can live up to it. Some women are good only in *one* room. Some are good only in *two* rooms. Others are good in all three rooms. Wonderful!

But what happens to the woman who is "not so hot" in the bedroom (according, of course, to the popular sex books)? Is she to be discarded? Is she not a worthwhile human being regardless? The value of a person does not lie in his or her expertness in the sexual realm.

Well, you may say, she can learn! Yes, she can be taught (depending on her psychological makeup), and there *are* many books around. She can also take a leaf out of the diaries of the sensuous women in history and with courage equip herself with the tricks and techniques and modes of self-display which once belonged to the prostitute, but which now belong to "nice people" such as daughters, sisters, sweethearts, and wives.

However, not all people have the courage to behave sexually as the popular books indicate they *should*. Perhaps they were inculcated as children with certain beliefs and sexual guilt feelings, which prevent them from yielding to their natural instincts, and now cause problems in their sexual lives. Statements such as, "Men are animals. Sex is dirty. Nice girls don't do that. A man will lose respect for you," can cause sexual hang-ups. Marriage counseling may help considerably in this instance.

Too much emphasis on sex is unrealistic. For some people, sex once in a while is enough—for others, no amount is enough. No book can tell you how often you *should* have sex. Some people place sex at the top of their list of priorities—others place it at the bottom. Both are normal. With advancing years the sexual drive may diminish and nonsexual joys begin to head the list. This is not to say that people cannot enjoy sex well into a ripe old age, provided the partners are healthy, willing, and available.

On the other hand, I know many couples who have a sexless marriage because of the inability of one or both partners to have sexual relations. One partner may be taking certain medications that may diminish the sexual drive. But, whatever their reasons, they have the utmost respect and affection for each other. As long as *both* partners feel that there are other joys in life—nonsexual joys—it is quite possible for them to maintain a pleasant and close relationship. The marriage can still be meaningful and happy if there is enough love and understanding.

I know other couples who had a very satisfactory sex life, but who had nothing else in common with each other. Communication was poor. There was no mutual encouragement or praise, and each was quick to point out the other's faults. Neither one could give any *emotional nourishment*. All they had was sex. And when the sex drive diminished, they were divorced. There was nothing else to keep the marriage going. So sex is not enough!

You can study all the sex manuals, learn a hundred different ways to have sex, but if you don't know how to reach your partner with a kind word, your expertise in the sexual realm won't work for you. Henry and Myrna, both fifty-two, had been married for six months when they moved into their new home. Prior to that they had no sexual problems —everything was fine. Henry's first marriage had ended in divorce, Myrna was a widow. Shortly after they moved into their new home, sexual problems developed. Myrna quickly bought all the sex books she could find to learn new techniques, but nothing worked. How could it? He had been getting a psychic beating constantly since they moved in. He felt inadequate. "I just want you to know," Myrna said the first day they were in their new home, "that if it weren't for my money we wouldn't be here." A few weeks later, as the last of the new furniture was being delivered, she said, "You know, if it weren't for my money this furniture wouldn't be here." The day the new color television set was delivered, she kept right on rubbing it in. "If it weren't for my money, this television set wouldn't be here." Henry could no longer take it. He decided to "fix" her, and so, very calmly, he said, "Myrna, I think you ought to know something. If it weren't for your money, *I* wouldn't be here."

Respect for one's spouse, kind, loving words, understanding—these things "turn on" a partner. These things make the sex act ecstatic. Love cannot be treated casually and yet remain a burning flame. Your heart is part of your body and your heart has feelings, too. Sex begins in the mind, travels to the genital organs, and ends with the heart if one is in love. Some people feel that sex need not be a commitment nor an expression of love. In other words, sex is not to be taken seriously. It is to be engaged in purely for fun. Certainly, sex should be fun; however, for many people, sex represents a bond, a commitment, a profound source of intimacy.

If I were able to give women only one sentence of advice as to how to keep their husbands or lovers in love with them I would choose this one: Let him know in words that he is the greatest and best, and the words, vitalized by love, will cause him to become so in fact. Positive words appeal to the emotions; they stay in the memory when the man or woman is alone. If a man wants to keep his wife in love with him, he must not only be a "lover," he must tell her in words and in manner how much she means to him and whenever he is pleased about anything. The woman's desire for loving words arises from a very natural cause. If the thought of love is there, there should be the words to express it. A woman's soul craves assurance. Hence the eternal question, "Do you love me?" Men should not be impatient with women who desire words of love.

One of the reasons some men hesitate to say "I love you" (even to their wives) is that their unconscious suggests caution. It says to them, in effect: "This female creature wants to trap you into an avowal of weakness for her—be on your guard." The man who is intelligent and generous enough to conquer his own instinct for caution because of his desire to give pleasure to the woman will live in joy. He lets her know by words and inferences that he adores her. He makes her feel that in his eyes *she* is the greatest, especially in bed (and so, she will become). And so, I again say, sex is not enough. Women—and men—want more!

SEXUALITY VS. GENITAL SEX

If one has to abstain from sexual intercourse for whatever reason, one can still experience sexuality. Psychological investigation indicates that sexuality is a great power in human life if handled properly. *It can be a great blessing when it is not misused.* Sexuality manifests itself in sensual sensations. For example: cuddling, touching, kissing, physical closeness, tenderness, and affection—any kind of pleasurable sensation is sexuality. Enjoying a particular kind of food, smacking your lips, devouring the food, is sexuality. Some people go to *extremes,* however. When one overeats or overdrinks or smokes too much he is misusing his sexuality. There are people who are never without something in their mouths—a cigarette, a drink, candy, gum, food—or they talk incessantly (you can't shut them up). The mouth keeps going all the time.

Sexuality knows no age. As long as we are alive we can experience sexuality. Deriving a great deal of pleasure from dancing is sexuality; enjoyment of one's work is sexuality; scintillating conversation is sexuality. Finding pleasure in making love even though it does not lead to orgasm is sexuality. Pleasure is pleasure whether it is pleasure of the mind or pleasure of the body.

One who is said to have "charisma" or "personal magnetism" radiates sexuality. Almost everybody is attracted to a sensuous personality. To some people, however, being sensuous means solely the ability to carry out sexual relations with flair and apparent ease. Sexual intercourse is only one facet of sexuality. True sexuality is an expression of the *total* personality.

More important than genital sex itself is the physical closeness and the companionship of sex. A gentle touch, holding each other, a word of endearment—these things help to satisfy the sexual instinct. The sex life of an individual is not confined to the bedroom. Sexuality is the opiate of the young and old. Wanting physical closeness is just as appropriate in the later years as in the earlier years. It is a drive throughout life. Sexuality will always be with us. It is a vital factor in life. It does not always relate to sexual intercourse.

Some people eat extraordinary amounts of food to compensate for their sexual frustration. If they don't get their sexual needs satisfied, they will get it another way. Overeating is not the best way. It's misusing sexuality and it's too fattening. Choose another form of sexuality—one that does not contain calories, yet is pleasurable. The solution of the sexual problem lies within the scope of every human being.

Phillip, a retired accountant, asked me to speak on sex and guilt feelings as I walked into class one day. In fact, he met me at the door and whispered it to me. He is seventy-two, a widower, and his girl friend, a widow, who is sixty-eight, is also in my class. She cooks for him every evening. They even have lunch together every day, but she wouldn't let him touch her physically. This has been going on for five months.

"She insists on marriage—no premarital sex or 'fooling around,' " he said. "I'm very fond of her," he added. "In fact, I may even be in love with her, but I want to sample the merchandise first. At my age I'd like to have a sample—I would like to find out if she is sexually responsive, though she claims to be in love with me. I'm still okay," he added, with a twinkle in his eyes. "But I don't know why she feels so guilty about premarital sex at her age. Please give us a talk on sex, Dr. Rose," he said.

Well, somehow, sex is not the easiest subject to discuss in some of my classes. Many of my students in their late sixties and early seventies have the erroneous belief that they are through sexually because one spouse may have said to the other, "Why don't you act your age? You should be through with that foolishness now." These destructive remarks may result in impotency.

The *fear* of becoming sexually impotent is the most painful fear of all to some males, and a husband or lover may rationalize that he's tired or doesn't feel well (the "I have a headache tonight" bit). It's a terrible burden for an older man to be put to the test every time he goes to bed with a woman. A woman can fake an orgasm, but as we all know, a man can't fake an erection. Some men actually become frightened and break off with a woman when they sense the woman is expecting a "performance."

At any rate, as I began to speak on the subject of sex, a man in his late sixties said in a bored tone, "Oh, let's talk about something else, Dr. Rose, what was, was." I then indicated that "what was" could still be, but in a *different form,* and that sexual responsiveness has no age limit. "Let's leave sex to youth," he said. What a devitalizing myth! This myth has caused much loneliness and frustration to many older people.

On the other hand, some couples in my classes in their late seventies and early eighties are the most sensuous couples I have ever had the pleasure of knowing. They don't look their age—they are vital, alive, they are *young.* Apparently the brain and a person's hands are the greatest sexual organs. They also subscribe to the old adage: "Use it or lose it."

Getting back to Phillip and his girl friend, I deliberately directed my talk along certain lines, hoping to reach home with her. For example, I indicated that what is reality for a young girl growing up is no longer the same reality for the woman in her sixties. Times have changed and we need to change our values sometimes to fit new situations in order to grow and go forward. It seems that the talk made an impression on his girl friend (I must have hit home) because when they came back to class the following week, he winked at me. They were married two weeks later.

One of my clients, a woman of seventy, beautiful in face

and form, and a widow for about one year, had suffered for six months from almost constant nausea. During our private session she indicated that her medical doctor had taken all kinds of tests and could find nothing organically wrong with her. He suggested she see a psychotherapist. She told me she met a man to whom she felt sexually attracted. She had been so horrified at the idea, so "nauseated" at what she considered a "sin," that she put it out of her mind.

What she actually did was to repress the desire. She put it into her unconscious, where it continued to function unsatisfied. Her nausea was the symbol of a moral disgust, which was converted into a physical nausea.

She felt too "refined" to be moved by any such sensual urge, especially since it was inculcated in her as a young girl, "Nice girls have sex only when they are married." But the strong sensual feeling within her toward this man would not be put down. Her guilt feelings were the result of a tyrannical conscience. "I'm a very passionate woman, Dr. Rose," she said. "Even at my age, I want sex and I'm ashamed of my feelings." "Your guilt is no longer relevant," I said. "You are no longer a young girl—you are seventy."

Somehow I had the feeling that she was also suffering from mental and emotional constipation. She was holding back—she wasn't giving out, and she was very uptight. It's difficult to help someone if the person holds back her thoughts and feelings.

"What happened with this man?" I asked her. "You say you are a passionate woman—what do you do about it?" "Well," she said, "I let him touch me a little here and there —and I touch him here and there—but I don't have intercourse—I wouldn't allow that." "Why not?" I asked. "Because I believe it's wrong unless one is married." "Your belief is knocking you out," I said. I then explained her conflict to her with the following story: Jimmy Durante was in a play in New York many years ago. In one of the scenes he puts on his hat and coat and takes them right off. A few minutes later he puts on his hat and coat again and takes them off again. This goes on for almost five minutes—on again, off again. Finally, he turns to the audience and says, "Did you ever have the feeling that you wanted to go and stay at the same time?"

"This is your conflict," I told my client. "You want to have sexual intercourse and you don't want to have sexual intercourse. Only *you* can resolve your conflict. It may help you to say to yourself, 'I no longer believe it is wrong to do that.' If you can convince yourself that it is no longer wrong at your age, you will be changing an infantile conscience into one which is more conducive to adult living and adult satisfactions."

After a few sessions in which she verbalized more guilt feelings, and my further explanations to her regarding her guilt (the voice of the conscience), her physical nausea disappeared. To treat guilt rationally, one must seek out the cause, think it through, and do whatever is necessary to alter or remove the cause.

The idea that older people are not interested in sex is a myth. Some grown children find it difficult for them to acknowledge that their parents are still engaging in sex. Older people who have an interesting and interested partner still engage in sexual intercourse or sexuality. A delightful couple in my class (he's seventy-four and she's seventy), told me when they go to bed they hold each other, cuddle, touch each other, but do not have genital sex (he can't). She's very happy just to be held. This is *their* sex. They are nourishing each other.

There are some people who have a sexual problem which is not related to physical causes or psychological causes, but rather to social causes. Single people—widows, widowers, divorced people—cannot always find a partner that they can relate to. They just don't meet anyone they really like well enough to cuddle with or have a satisfactory sexual relationship with. So they learn to live without sex, and without any ill effects, unless they *believe* the myth that "sexual intercourse is important for your health." It's the other way around—good health is important for sexual intercourse. If you are in poor health or tired all the time, you have no desire for sex.

If you are a single person and you have no partner to cuddle with, go to dances or find someone to take you dancing rather than to the movies. Dancing is a great expression of sexuality if you get pleasure out of it. The sexual instinct can be sublimated and dancing is one way. Accomplishing things is another way.

YOU CAN LIVE WITHOUT SEX (IF NECESSARY)

Sex researchers tell us that people who remain youthful are usually sexually active for a long time—into their seventies and eighties. However, suppose you don't have a sexual partner or for some other reason you no longer engage in sexual activity—will you age more rapidly? *No!* A thousand times, *no.* It is true that being loved and loving in return helps to keep one youthful—because you are *happy* —but that does not mean you must have genital sex. You can be happy through sublimation, too. Many older people no longer indulge in sexual intercourse and still look youthful. There are many nonsexual joys in life to keep one happy and youthful.

You *can* live without sex and remain healthy. You don't decrease your longevity if you don't have sex. It doesn't give you wrinkles either if you don't have sex. But if a person has a need for this form of intimacy or believes that he *must* have sex in order to be healthy physically and mentally and finds himself without a willing partner, then it may create emotional problems—not because of lack of sexual intimacy but because of the *belief* which causes the *frustration*. You can sublimate the frustration. When you sublimate, it merely means that you are diverting your sexual energy into other constructive and pleasurable activities. In order to compensate for the lack of sexual pleasure some people become very involved in good causes and do a lot of good in the world. Sublimation has always existed—it usually operates unconsciously. You get an urge to join a club, to do something constructive; you look for things to do that will eventually bring you recognition and gratification. When you put your sexual energy into some other form of activity that satisfies you, that's sublimation.

Sublimation is the story of my life. It has kept me healthy and happy. I love men—I think they're great—but I can't be a bed-hopper—that's not me. So I sublimate. I'm always involved in projects. Writing is a sublimation. I couldn't even handle a man now—all my sexual energy is going into this book right now. It gives me great pleasure. And as I stated before, pleasure is pleasure no matter which way you get it.

Sublimation is a form of adjustment. People who refuse to adjust through sublimation very often are unhappy and full of anxiety. Public speaking is a form of sublimation. Some actors and actresses who are no longer acting have turned to speech-making. They travel around giving lectures. They are "acting" in a different form.

Finding the *proper outlet* for our lack of sexual intimacy and other kinds of frustration keeps us healthy and young. It is as if to say, "I might as well accept this frustration in a calm manner and go on to something else that will give me satisfaction."

Some people have the attitude, "If I can't have the *real* thing I don't want anything else." This is a wrong attitude. Whether or not you accept the concept of sublimation, the inability or refusal to deal with disappointments and frustration keeps one tense and unhappy, and may produce illnesses. When we sublimate we get rid of hostile feelings and loneliness. We all have to sublimate because we can't always get what we want when we want it.

Men's clubs, women's clubs, and other civic organizations are all forms of sublimation. Someone gives you a pat on the back: "You did a great job, Ethel." "You're a terrific fund raiser, John." "Your speech was just wonderful, Belle." You're getting love. Perhaps you don't call it "love." But it is appreciation, affection, and acceptance. It sure beats going to bed with someone you don't care about just because you've heard that "sex is healthy." If you don't care about the person, it is *healthier* to sublimate. There is much more gratification.

If you never had sex again, nothing would happen to you. *Sexual energy does not have to be expressed sexually.* If you decide sublimation is the answer for you, you can still live a good life and derive youthful and healthful benefits.

FOR MEN ONLY: YOU'RE NOT WHAT YOU USED TO BE—SO WHAT?

Stop banging your head against a stone wall. You can't relive the earlier years. If you are in reasonably good health, nonuse is to blame for decline in sexual vigor. It may also be a cause for temporary impotency. Older unmarried men either repress their sex drive or just don't feel that it is worth the bother of looking for a sexual partner at "their" age. Losing interest in women means also losing interest in living.

An older married man may also repress his sex drive

because his wife is either unwilling to have sexual intercourse any longer or she may be ill.

The sex organ is a muscle—exercise it and it will keep on performing. Some men who have abstained from sex for a long period have a problem getting it started again; as in the case of Samuel, whose wife was ill for one year before she died. Six months after her death he started to date again. He was a very good-looking man of sixty and women were attracted to him. He was crushed when he discovered he just could not get an erection—especially when the woman he was with remarked, "I guess you're all used up." She didn't mean to be unkind—she was just tactless. If she understood the problem, she could have soothed him. She might have said, "Let's just have fun cuddling and touching. It doesn't matter—I'm just as happy to be with you. I like you. Perhaps in time it will happen." Samuel did not give up, however. He met another woman whom he could relate to and explained his "problem" this time. She was very understanding. He kept on "practicing" until he got it started again.

Temporary impotence in older men (or even younger men) is mainly psychological. You don't use sexuality up like a tube of toothpaste. The important thing is not to take sexual failures too seriously. It does *not* make you less of a man. Accept it for the time being and try to ascertain the cause. See your doctor first. If he finds no physical reason for your problem, it is purely *psychological*. Think about the following psychological factors which cause *temporary* impotence and see if any apply to you:

- Are you under emotional stress? Are you worried about something?
- Does your mate turn you off? If you are single, do other women turn you off? Ask yourself why.
- Do you consume too much alcohol prior to

making love? Alcohol is an enemy of sex for men in advanced years (and for some younger men, too). Too many men blame age when alcohol is the real culprit. I am reminded of Albert, a shy widower of sixty-two, who decided to go to a bar with the hope of meeting a woman. He found himself sitting next to a gorgeous woman of about fifty-five who was alone, too. Tongue-tied by her beauty (and extremely timid) he told the bartender he would pick up the bill for all her drinks. For about an hour he just sat and drank and admired her. Finally in desperation, encouraged by the vast amount of liquor he had consumed, he blurted out like a schoolboy, "Do you ever go to bed with men?" She gave him a warm smile and answered, "I never have before, but you just talked me into it, you silver-tongued devil!" The outcome of the story is: with all that liquor in him he couldn't do a damn thing. What a waste!

- Do you have an unconscious (or conscious) fear of failure in the bedroom? You may rationalize that you are too tired or you don't feel well. Don't deceive yourself.
- Are you worried about "performance?"
- Are you harboring a grudge toward your sex partner? You may even want to punish her unconsciously—so you punish her by failing sexually. Talk out anger—don't harbor grudges—it interferes with your sex life.
- Are you blaming your decline in sexual vigor or temporary impotence on age? There are changes in the physiological aspects of sex with age, but a man can still be sexually active

into the seventies, eighties, and even nineties. In other words, it takes longer for him to have an erection and he doesn't ejaculate as quickly as he used to, but this is not a hindrance in lovemaking. In fact, he is able to prolong his own enjoyment and that of his partner.
- Are you taking tranquilizers? The sexual drive diminishes when a man who is in reasonably good health, but full of tensions and anxieties, takes potent tranquilizers. Everything relaxes, including the penis—and especially that—it just sleeps and sleeps. Try using autosuggestion to calm yourself down instead of a tranquilizer. (See Chapter 1, autosuggestion). *Your brain is the greatest aphrodisiac.* Use it to talk to your penis—it will wake it up, encourage it to do its job, and then it can go back to sleep.
- Are you afraid of having a heart attack (a secret phobia) during the sex act? Even if a man has had a heart attack, usually when he is fully recovered his doctor will advise him to resume sexual relations. Some words of caution here. Do check with your own doctor, and do realize that having sex with a woman other than your wife may produce guilt. Tension and guilt may cause another heart attack, not the sex act itself.

I should like to remind you again that worries, your relationship with your wife at a certain period, a broken love affair (if you are single), divorce, loss of your spouse—all create fluctuations in your sexual life. Sometimes your sex drive will diminish for a week or months at a time and then return again. It depends on psychological factors. But do not lose interest in women because you are not what you used to be sexually.

It's Okay To Be Impotent

If you are on certain medications for high blood pressure or diabetes, this may be a cause for impotency. Ask your doctor about the kind of medication you are taking because some can cause impotence. Sometimes a different medication may have the same beneficial effect for your particular problem but not cause impotence. This is something you must work out with your doctor.

However, let's assume that nothing works and you are impotent—so? So what? No one ever died from impotency. You can still live. You are still a worthwhile human being and a man. If you permit yourself to be devastated by your impotence, the damage you will do to your health is far worse than not being able to have sexual intercourse. You can still experience "sexuality." What about physical closeness—lying side by side, holding each other, touching, kissing—isn't that important? What about nonsexual joys? There are so many things to do in this world.

Impotence is not a disgrace—it's a disgrace to withdraw from life when there are so many other pleasures.

ROMANCE AND SEX DO NOT BELONG TO YOUTH ALONE

I have some students in my classes who have been married for forty-five years and longer. They have told me privately that they still enjoy the sex act. For females, there's no age limit regarding sex; and as for the male, he, too, has the capacity for sexual performance well past the eighties if he is in good physical and psychological health. Regularity of sexual expression is important for maintaining sexual capacity. This is essential for both women and men.

This recreation is not limited to the young. Neither do you need special equipment. All you need is a caring and willing partner. Even though the husband may lose his hair and become paunchy and the wife may no longer be as slender as she once was and even have developed a few wrinkles, as long as they remain in love and concerned with each other's well-being and happiness, sexual enthusiasm will continue for a long time.

Attitude is everything. If you believe that you are through with sex past sixty, you won't be able to have sex. If you believe that you can, you will—as long as you are not suffering from any physical disease.

Recently I read in a Miami newspaper about a man of eighty and a woman of seventy-nine getting married. They went to one of the hotels on Miami Beach for their honeymoon. The new husband insisted that the twin beds be taken out and replaced with a king-size bed. They brought along a popular sex book and stayed up most of the night reading (and practicing) page by page. What zest for living these two people have!

It warms my heart to see some of my students (husbands and wives in their sixties and seventies) holding hands while I am lecturing. Romance has kept them youthful. They are more "alive" than some younger people I know. Pauline, one of my students who is only sixty, was worried about her friend Charlotte, who is sixty-seven. Charlotte took up dancing lessons and it seemed that she was in love with her thirty-year-old dancing instructor. "She's gone haywire with romance," Pauline said. "I think she needs help badly. I'm going to bring her to class next week—please talk to her for a few minutes." The moment Charlotte walked into the classroom the light seemed to get brighter

—she was dazzling. The difference between the two women was amazing. Pauline at sixty looked seventy. She had had no interest in men since her husband died; in fact, she had no interest in anything. Charlotte, a widow only nine months, looked no more than fifty-five. I was very much impressed with her and in speaking with her I discovered that she had loved her husband so much, that the first month after he died she thought of suicide. Attempting to help herself, she read all kinds of things on how to deal with grief. Nothing seemed to help her much until she came across a quote by Alfred Tennyson, the English poet, "I must lose myself in action lest I wither in despair." This was her antidote for her grief, she said. She lost herself in "action." She looked for activities which gave her pleasure. She kept busy. It was sink or swim, she said. She loved dancing and so she took some lessons; and because the dance studio ran socials she bought herself long flowing dresses and every time she danced with the instructor she felt like Ginger Rogers. She happened to mention this casually to her friend. She also indicated that the instructor made her feel like a "woman" again, which manifested itself in other areas of her life. She found life to be beautiful again. It wasn't that she was "in love" with the instructor—she was just enjoying her life and was blossoming. Pauline thought it was outrageous—false eyelashes, coloring her hair, carrying on as if she were eighteen. Charlotte was really to be admired. She no longer needed tranquilizers—she was calm and relaxed as she spoke. She would not permit Pauline to discourage her. Pauline was sinking and didn't know it. Both women made choices consciously or unconsciously. Pauline chose to sink—Charlotte chose to live.

No, romance does not belong to youth alone. Ruth, a lovely woman in her late seventies, confessed in class one day that she and her eighty-year-old husband went on a cruise recently and made love like mad. Everyone thought they were newlyweds (they've been married over fifty years). She also added, "If anyone in this class thinks sex is only for the young, he's crazy or lying to himself because he hasn't got the right partner."

A former client of mine, a woman of sixty-eight, married a man her own age. Sally had a beautiful face and a sparkling personality. She was quite plump, however—too plump. Her new husband was a handsome retired engineer. They were delighted to have found each other. She cooked gourmet meals, which he loved; she redecorated his home because he wanted it to reflect *her* personality. She floated about in flowing caftans and chiffon peignoirs. They were blissfully happy. They made love in the dark only because she didn't want him to see her flabby body nude or her varicose veins. He accepted her explanation that she was "modest."

One day, the thought occurred to Sally that perhaps she should be *more* romantic—look sexier. And so, one day, having read a popular book that deals with "costumes that will enhance your lovemaking," she greeted her husband at the door when he returned from playing golf draped in Saran Wrap. "Hi, darling . . . surprised?" He was horrified. He had never seen her body in broad daylight. He was so shocked and turned off he could not respond sexually. But because he truly loved her, he sat her down (he covered her with a sheet first—Saran Wrap sticks to your fanny), and had a talk with her. "Dear," he said, "at your age, you don't have to wrap yourself in Saran Wrap to entice me. I am turned on when I see you floating around in a chiffon peignoir. I am turned on by the fragrance that emanates from your body. I am turned on when you serve me a gourmet meal because I know you cooked it with love. I am turned on when I observe you at a party; how people are drawn to you. I am turned on when you say to me, 'What can I do for you?—I love you so.' "

Sally learned that different men require different things to turn them on. Saran Wrap may be okay for very young women who have terrific bodies, but at age sixty-eight and beyond, it's sexier to wear a peignoir or anything else that camouflages the flabbiness and varicose veins. Sally's husband had sexual fantasies when she floated around in her beautiful caftans, but he was also very realistic outside of bed.

A widower told me that the widows and divorcees in his condominium do not leave him alone. One widow of about sixty-five rang his bell at 7:30 one morning dressed in a shortie nightgown (but all made up), and asked if she could borrow the morning newspaper. He told her the only way she could read his paper was in his bed. She fled and never bothered him again. Another recent widower told me the women in his building want to "console" him. They keep bringing him chicken soup. He is so full of chicken soup he is thinking of moving out of the building. Widowers and divorced men who are not *ready* for a sexual relationship seem to be appalled by aggressive tactics. When the emotional pain has subsided and they reconnect with life again, usually *they* make the sexual overtures; as one man told me, "I'm ready now for a woman whose hobbies are cooking and making love."

Looking for a new mate can be compared to shopping for clothes. You pick the garment you like best, take it home—hoping it suits you. If you find you used poor judgment in choosing the garment, you have an option. You can either bring it back and forget about it, exchange it, or you can tell yourself, "Oh, well, I'll keep it and not torture myself and try to be as happy as I can with it."

How to Live with a Retired Husband

9

Your children may love their father very much, but they have their own lives to lead and their own problems, so don't burden your children by complaining, "Your father is driving me nuts." Don't even complain to your friends, "My husband is driving me up the wall." They can't help you. You will have to work it out yourself and you can do it.

Your husband's retirement can be quite disturbing to you. It's understandable. If your husband did not prepare himself for retirement mentally and emotionally, if he did not develop new interests and hobbies, if he is inactive (though in reasonably good health) and just hangs around the house all day, if he tells you he's "too old" to try something new, if he interferes with your pleasures, it is not uncommon for marital problems to develop. A retired man can be a burden to his wife. Having her husband around all day long can be emotionally and physically exhausting to a woman who is accustomed to freedom most of the day. Don't become upset and frustrated, don't develop psychosomatic symptoms—there *are* ways to handle the situation. You can make your husband's retirement a beautiful adventure for both of you.

First, bear in mind that he feels useless now. He needs a great deal of encouragement at this point in his life. Most retired men do not want to vegetate, at least consciously.

Some men, however, feel that they have worked hard enough in their earlier years and now they have a right to do nothing. But after a while these men begin to lean heavily on their wives for companionship. Some wives have said to me, "When I'm about to leave the house for a bridge game, my husband says, 'Where are you going? When will you be back? What am I supposed to do while you are gone?' I don't want to be pinned down to a time. It makes me feel tense and guilty knowing he's alone with nothing to do, and so I don't go—I stay with him." If your husband is not in ill health, giving him sympathy is a mistake. *Do not feed his self-pity.* He needs all the love and kindness that you can muster, yes—but sympathy, no. If your husband wants to fritter away his life piecemeal, it doesn't mean that you have to, also. If he wants to commit psychological suicide, you don't have to follow him. *You go to the bridge game!* Being restricted from doing your thing will only lead to antagonism toward your husband. You don't have to stagnate, too. You don't have to retire from life because he did.

Have a talk with him. If you already have, try again. Suggest that he take up fishing, golfing, painting, sculpturing, or volunteer work, get a part-time job, anything that will get him out of the house. But most importantly his *mind* must be busy. A few of my male students (at my suggestion) took up sculpturing. They made the most beautiful things—animals in bronze, busts of famous men. These men had never worked with their hands before. They were thrilled and full of enthusiasm. Two of the men are in their seventies—and they now look younger, act younger, have become younger! This is what can happen to a person when his zest for living comes back—he's revitalized.

If your husband does not appreciate your suggestions and you cannot persuade him to do something, do not become discouraged or angry. Do not say things which you may be sorry for afterward. Ask yourself, "Will this statement I'm about to make lift him up or tear him down?" For that matter, we can ask the same question with regard to ourselves. "Are my thoughts making me feel good or am I making myself feel bad? Am I feeding myself hope, optimistic thoughts, or despair?" Just continue to do what you want to do—whether it's taking a course in adult education or going out with the women to lunch. The life you save will have to be your own. You have a right to make the most of your life. If your husband wants to rust, that's too bad, but you don't have to be punished. Of course, if your husband is ill and needs you at home all day, that's unfortunate, but not catastrophic. It can still be worked out. One of my students has a sick husband. She has arranged for a nurse's aide to come in for four hours every day. Once a week she comes to my class and the rest of the week she does other things that distract her from her problem for a few hours each day. She returns home rejuvenated. She is preserving her sanity.

PROMISES, PROMISES, PROMISES

"When we were planning to move to Florida," Susan told me, "my husband promised me I would have a lot of time for myself, that I could do the things I'd always wanted to do but couldn't when I was rearing my children. It didn't turn out that way at all. I'm busier now with him than I ever was. He eats ten times a day—I can't seem to get out of the kitchen. When I finally get out for a while I have to watch the clock and run home to give him lunch. He doesn't even know how to make a sandwich or boil an egg." I couldn't believe that Susan's husband didn't know how to make a sandwich. I asked Susan if she really wanted to feel "needed" and unconsciously enjoyed having her husband dependent on her. If it wasn't so, then Susan should teach him how to fix his own lunch or let him eat lunch out. She could take him into the kitchen and show him how to put two slices of cheese between two slices of bread. Now, any *child* can do that. My grandson did it at age four. If you don't want to keep your husband a child, tell him you have faith in him, that he won't starve, that he is capable of fixing something for himself. He may not like it; he may say it tastes much "better" when you make it. Don't feel guilty. You can always fix it, if you wish, put it in the refrigerator and say, "Your lunch is in the refrigerator, dear. I have to leave."

We all have heard the expression, "I married him for better or worse but not for lunch." It's not really serving a husband lunch that bothers a woman—it's his hanging around the house all day and not doing anything useful that gets on her nerves.

Another wife complained to me, "My husband promised me when he retired we would do things *together.* He would go with me to museums, take walks with me (I don't like walking alone), take courses in adult education with me, go to different places. But he gets up early and leaves the house with his golf clubs and I don't see him again until dinner time. He comes home tired, eats, watches TV, and goes to sleep. What do you do with a husband like that?" What do you do with a parent who breaks promises to a child? The child loses confidence in the parent after a while. Assert yourself. Express your feelings in a calm way, with no shouting. You might say something like this: "I feel resentful. You haven't kept one promise to me. I didn't nag you when you were very active in business. I knew you needed all the rest you could get. You have earned the right to play golf every day and eat lunch with your golf friends. You even have the right to break a few promises, but I feel that you should keep your word on *some* of the promises you made to me. I am finding it difficult to believe you now when you tell me next week or next month we will do this or that.

You don't follow through." This manner of asserting yourself will at least let your husband know what your feelings are, and perhaps he will show more consideration. But more importantly, you have *expressed* your anger constructively, which is healthy for *you*. If you hold your anger in, it will deplete your energy and possibly induce psychosomatic symptoms. Other women are very happy when their husbands aren't under their feet all day.

Another wife told me her husband has varied interests and is busy all day. She, too, is busy during the day—she does *her* thing. They are both very happy. Evenings they do things together. They have worked out things mutually. If you have the kind of husband that has looked forward to doing all the things he has always wanted to do and is now doing them, you will have to find some meaningful activities on your own if you can't share your husband's activities. Neither spouse should be dependent on the other for amusement. Just as you can't always provide stimulation for your husband, neither can he always provide stimulation for you. There *are* things you can do together, however—concerts, plays, movies, dancing, socializing.

THE PRESIDENT OF THE KITCHEN

Some retired husbands want to be helpful in terms of the home, so they start changing things around. A man does not want to lose the authority role that he once had in business, so now he transfers it to the kitchen. For forty years he never knew what the kitchen looked like and now he is telling you how to rearrange the pots and pans, the glasses, the silverware, how to cook, how the dishes should be washed, and so on. In short, he has become the president of the kitchen. You don't have to get upset, you have a choice.

You can let him be the president of the kitchen and assume *all* responsibilities, which include marketing and cooking and cleaning up after meals, or if you do not wish to give up your presidential position, you can tell him to go find his own job. One of my students who had this kind of a problem (every time she looked for a pot or a glass, it was in a different place) finally conceded. She let her husband take over the presidency of the kitchen and he is sorry he did. After she has eaten, she walks away from the table and sits down to read or watch television while the president cleans up. She refuses to take back her job. She is waiting until he really gets his fill of it. In the meantime she has a respite from the work and feels like *she* has retired for a while.

Husbands who are living in the past should say to themselves, "What I used to be or do doesn't matter anymore—what can I do *now* to make the rest of my life worthwhile?" If he looks upon retirement as the beginning of a new life, if he opens up a new door—a door to a magnificent, wonderful new life—he becomes recharged.

Keeping busy has many definitions. Your husband may rationalize that he *is* keeping busy, but actually he may be just killing time. If that is true, he may become a hypochondriac. It's not a disease in itself—he's only worried about a disease he may get or a disease that hasn't even been invented yet. It is strictly a defense. He doesn't have to seek new activities now and he doesn't have to take you out ("Can't you see I'm sick?"). He has an exaggerated anxiety about his health. Little pains (whether they are real or imagined) become big pains. Don't feed your husband's hypochondria if he complains about minor ailments—it won't make him better. Suggest he see his doctor. Perhaps you can convince him that there is nothing organically wrong with him. You may also point out to your husband that other persons in your community who *are* in poor health are still enjoying their lives nonetheless because they refuse to decay from idleness.

If your husband becomes slovenly in appearance (which sometimes happens because of boredom), remind him of the psychological benefits of good grooming. "Dressing up" makes one feel good. If your husband is in reasonably good health and he wants you to wait on him hand and foot, he has regressed (he's not senile yet). Regression means going back to childish behavior. It's very common. It manifests itself in temper tantrums, sulking, etc. In other words, when he doesn't get his way he acts like a child of five. Remind him that he's a grown man, not a child. A grown man talks out grievances—he doesn't sulk or give his spouse the silent treatment.

If your husband is rigid, understand that you can't move him. He is inflexible. He adheres to one philosophy—his own. He will avoid situations that call for flexibility. Even when driving with him in his car, if you tell him, "Honey, take this route to Jack's house—it's shorter," he will stick to *his* route because he is rigid. He is not willing to experiment. No sense in your becoming irritated. Just accept it—look the other way. The other alternative is for you to be tense, anxious, and resentful. Is that going to make him less rigid? No. But you practice flexibility on your own. You keep on doing things differently so that you don't become rigid. Break the chain of routine.

Your husband may start blaming you for his unhappiness. "If you were different, if you were this or that, I would be different or things would be different." Hogwash! He is using a defense mechanism called "projection," which means to blame someone else for one's own failures, inadequacies, or whatever. It's too painful emotionally to blame himself for his inactivity, his unhappiness, so his wife is the handy target. I have known husbands to blame their wives when they failed in business. One wife, whose husband never discussed his business affairs with her, didn't even know how her husband's business was run. When she asked simple questions regarding his business he would reply, "Do I interfere with your running the home? Don't interfere in my business." When he failed (because of poor judgment) he blamed her for the failure. The kids drove him wild... She didn't cook gourmet meals... She didn't do this ... She didn't do that... This projection saved his face. It's too painful for some men to admit their inadequacies, so the wife "gets it." Projection saves the retired man's face, too, if he has retired to "nothingness." Don't feel guilty. Understand that he is projecting when he blames you for things that have nothing to do with you personally. Should you keep quiet and just "take it"? No. There's no sense in giving him hell—that won't solve his problem. But you might say to him, "I'm not to blame for your lack of desire or inability to adjust to retirement. If you wish to use me as the scapegoat, it will not help you one bit. Quit fooling yourself. You'll have to learn to adjust to new circumstances. I'll help you if you let me, but I cannot help you if you blame me and refuse to be helped." You might also add that his old philosophy is no longer useful and that he needs to develop a new philosophy for dealing with retirement.

Perhaps you can get your husband to identify with other retirees, those who are active, enjoying life, and taking their wives out. Invite them to your home. Positive identification is a form of adjustment. If he could identify with someone whom he himself admires, it is as if he becomes the other person. He begins to think and behave like the other person. He learns from him. Positive identification is valuable for both young and older people. For instance, when one identifies with a great person, one strives to become great, too. When you watch a movie and you identify with the hero or heroine, you feel what he or she feels. If she cries, you cry —if she laughs, you laugh. Sometimes you walk out of a theater or movie emulating the hero or heroine. Your husband may have some negative identifications with other retirees who do nothing—men who just complain and talk about ailments and how life is mistreating them.

If your husband doesn't hear well, he may use that as an excuse not to mingle with others. It's nothing to be ashamed of. Ask friends to speak louder. Sometimes the person who does not hear well either shouts when he speaks and then feels embarrassed or speaks so low (especially if he is wearing a hearing aid), people can't hear *him* so there's no communication and he loses self-confidence. Make up a code with him. When he speaks too loudly, you will start patting your hair. If he speaks too low, you will rub your hands together. Make up any kind of a code and practice it at home until he becomes accustomed to your signals. This may induce him to socialize more.

Only *he* can make his retirement successful. Each man must decide for himself what will give him the most satisfaction and what will make him feel that life is still wonderful. Two thousand years ago, Seneca said, "No man can be great or powerful that is not master of himself."

Zest for living increases longevity. The elixir of life is keeping busy. If your husband refuses to cultivate the will to live and is behaving in a self-destructive manner, you cultivate *your* will to live. The body chemistry responds to the will to live. Refuse to be dragged down by his self-defeating behavior.

HOW TO SAVE YOUR SANITY WHILE LIVING WITH A RETIRED HUSBAND

- Do not neglect your own appearance. You owe it to yourself to look your best.
- Remember that you're not out to hurt him, but you have a right to go after happiness.
- Don't make too many demands on him. You both need time to adjust to retirement.

- Greet every day with enthusiasm.
- Do not rust along with your husband. Do the things *you* want to do regardless of him.
- If you are discouraged, think of it as a temporary mood. Tell yourself, "I'll get over it soon." And do something to lift up your spirits.
- Don't hate him for being underfoot. He needs to find himself—he's lost.
- Your influence over your husband may be limited but there is nothing to stop you from changing yourself. Your emotional reaction to his behavior is under *your* control. Whether you should react kindly, selfishly, compassionately, cruelly is your choice. Choose to have serenity instead of frustration, harmony instead of disharmony.
- Hang a little blackboard on *his* closet door and label it *Complaints*. For example" "Darling, you dropped your wet bathing suit on the carpet again. Please remember to drop it in the laundry basket." Or, "Sweetheart, does your golf bag have to lay on the bedroom floor? I nearly fell over it. Please put it into your closet." Don't erase the complaints until they are taken care of. If you need more than one blackboard, get it. (Let him get his own blackboard for his complaints). Don't waste energy yelling or screaming. Some people are more visually minded. Things seem to sink in better when they read them.
- If your husband keeps telling you, "Darling, you should wash it this way or you should do it that way (who knows, he may become president of the laundry room, too), tell him that you belong to a club that has rules and you

only do things his way on the days that the club rules permit it. He will get the message (hopefully).
- Above all, don't lose hope. He may wake up one morning and decide that he, too, wants to get the best out of life.
- Take every opportunity to extend your mental involvement.
- Realize that he may become insecure because you refuse to lose your zest for life. He may even envy you secretly because you are growing. You might say something like this: "I love you, but I love life, too, and I want to live it fully."
- You will save your sanity. I'll bet on you because you know that life must be lived whether your husband is in favor of it or not.

How to Heal Psychological Wounds

10

Be calm, and strong, and patient. Meet failure and disappointment with courage. Rise superior to the trials of life, and never give in to hopelessness or despair.
Dr. William Osler

Most people have suffered psychological injuries at one time or another. Everyone has been frustrated, rejected, discouraged, disappointed, and experienced sorrow. These are all psychological wounds which can be treated very effectively by psychological methods.

But sometimes a psychological injury leaves a scar that affects the person's life to such an extent that he or she becomes a recluse.

One of my students brought a friend to class one day. They both sat in the first row and I could see that the friend was crying. During a five-minute break I asked her if I could help in some way. She began to sob even more. "I can't get over the death of my husband," she managed to squeeze out between sobs. The way she carried on, I thought he had died the day before. At any rate, I asked her how long it had been. "Five years," she said. This woman was no longer suffering from grief—she was suffering from self-pity. To grieve for five years is an abnormal reaction. This is not to say that one forgets the loved one—it's a matter of *adjustment.* In order to survive emotionally, one *must* sublimate the grief. One must find ways to save one's own life. A live corpse is worse than a dead one. We all have the power within us to help ourselves, if we want to, and that's a big *if.* Some people just want the whole world to feel sorry for them. Sympathy is negative. It makes a person feel worse and weaker emotionally. It says, in effect: "You poor thing, I don't know how you can live through it. I don't know how you can take this." Empathy is positive. Empathy says, "I understand how you feel—I understand your 'hurt.' But you will surmount it—you are indestructible."

There are many kinds of psychological wounds. But not everyone responds the same way to an unpleasant experience. One person may be crushed by rejection and another may slough it off. Some people get sick from frustration and others take it in their stride. Reality is what it is and not what you would like it to be. Since there's no escape from reality, you might as well deal with it rationally. An emotionally stable person can take a lot of frustration and rejection even though he may not like it. He faces it and comes out a winner. An immature person gets defeated by the slightest frustration or rejection. When we have confidence in our ability to take frustration we don't get anxieties if what we set out to do does not work out. If we are afraid that we may not be able to handle the situation, we feel anxious and tense.

The world is too full of sadness, sorrow, misery, and sickness; it needs more sunshine; it needs cheerful people; it needs people who encourage, not discourage; it needs people who lift up, not tear down. Who can estimate the value of such people—people who radiate good cheer wherever they go instead of gloom and sadness. The ability to radiate sunshine is a greater power than mere physical beauty. It's possible for everyone to acquire this inestimable gift. It comes from within—it comes from the way we think and perceive life.

ANTIDOTES FOR PSYCHOLOGICAL WOUNDS

- Pour some psychological iodine on your emotional wound before the infection turns to hatred or depression. You can't buy this iodine in a drug store. Healing an emotional injury is an *inside job*. No pill or booze will do it for you. The cure lies within you. Psychological iodine consists of constructive thinking—rational thinking. Change your attitude toward the person or situation and your injury will heal.
- Reshape your life. Do something each day that gives you a little pleasure.
- Don't dwell on your emotional hurts. It cannot help you; it will only perpetuate the hurts.
- Don't withdraw from people because you fear rejection again. Rejection cannot injure you or scar you if your attitude is right.
- Don't pretend to be strong. *Be* strong.
- Take every resentment, every grudge you are harboring, every fear, every rejection, and throw them all in the garbage pail. That's where they belong—not in your mind. The way to get rid of psychological enemies is to clean out the mind.

- Be cheerful. Nobody likes to be with a grumbler or a fault-finder.
- Develop a sense of humor. It's a terrific first-aid tool.
- Be optimistic. *You* will be encouraged and you will infect others with your optimism.
- Poise is the enemy of anxiety. The more poise you develop the less wounded you will feel.
- Adapt yourself to any situation. Should someone use you as a scapegoat, instead of getting angry, feel compassion for that person. He's in pain and you know how it feels to be in emotional pain.
- Don't lose your rational, healing power for one moment. It is your most important first-aid tool for psychological injuries.
- Expect to have fun; expect to be serene. It *is* possible to better your life.
- Remember, no day is rotten—it's just that some days are better than others.

It's Time to Live a New Life

11

> *How essential it is ... to be able to live inside a mind, with attractive and interesting pictures on the walls.*
> William Lyon Phelps

You have reached the second or third part of your life—the magnificent fifties, the glorious sixties, the noble seventies. Ahead of you still lie years of useful activity and splendid health. These years should be your most rewarding. Reach out and take what life has to offer. Don't let anyone or anything hold you back from beginning a new life. People *can* change their lives. Millions of people have done it—so can you.

Here's how some of my students started a new life: Jacob, a retired businessman of sixty-five, went back to college to earn a law degree. He doesn't know as yet what he will do afterward, but it has been his dream to be a lawyer.

Selma, a grandmother of fifty-nine, decided she wanted a high school diploma. She is attending evening classes and will get her diploma soon. Celia, a grandmother of sixty, is a college freshman. She is majoring in psychology. This has been her dream. Sandra, sixty-four, always wanted to be an actress. Now that she is a widow and all of her five children are married, she decided to do what she always longed to.

She puts on plays at temples and churches, acts in them, directs them—she's having a ball. She seeks out opportunities to "act." She puts on skits in her own condominium, too. She gets everyone involved in the skits. These people are in their late sixties and seventies—they never dreamed they would become actors and actresses at their age. Sandra made up her mind that she would not become a pain-in-the-neck to her children, so she began a new life. Joseph and Ethel, in their sixties, just opened a boutique shop to keep busy.

Sophie, sixty-two, took up painting two years ago. She now sells her paintings to the people in her community. Because of her expertise in bridge, Hilda, seventy, has had many requests to teach it. She now conducts classes in bridge in her home for a nominal fee. Mary, fifty-eight, always wanted to be a model. Since her figure is still good, she went to modeling school and now models clothes for the "older" woman. Mary, incidentally, is sublimating her grief. She never thought she could stop wallowing in self-pity.

Your children and friends will admire you for your courage to begin anew. A new life can involve a second career or it can be anything you want. If you don't need the money, you may wish to volunteer your services. Community organizations, hospitals, and other kinds of agencies need you.

Don't expect to stay young by just moping around the house or watching television all day. You must have some mental exercise. Go to libraries, read books and magazines. One of my students has an electric personality—when she talks about what she has read she inspires everyone around her to dash out and buy the book or magazine. You can cure boredom. Keep your mind active and force yourself to keep busy. If you don't use your mind and body, you will vegetate. Start using your muscles so that they don't atrophy and waste away.

THE BEST IS YET TO COME

Does thou love life? Then do not squander time, for that is the stuff life is made of.

Benjamin Franklin

When life is very interesting for us, we want to live. We cultivate the "will to live" instinct. Do you have one or more unfulfilled desires deep down in your heart? It's not too late to attempt to realize them. Perhaps your inferiorities have held you back all these years. Perhaps you were afraid to take whatever risks were necessary to achieve your goal. What have you got to lose now? This inextinguishable fire inside you can torture you if you don't start working on fulfilling some of your dreams. As long as your goals are realistic and you do something each day that will bring you closer to your dreams, you will make it. Don't be impatient—just work steadily toward the realization of your dreams. Plan your life as if you were going to live another fifty years. You may say, "But I have no patience now. I'm tired, I'm too old . . ." If you feel that you are too tired to start a new life, too tired to climb your Mt. Everest, your thinking has to be changed. Unless you are in very poor health, your thoughts are keeping you exhausted. Perhaps you lack confidence in your ability. How will you reach your Mt. Everest if you are fearful and have lost confidence in yourself? Whatever your Mt. Everest is, you have to climb it yourself—no one else can do it for you. When you are no longer afraid to take risks, when you are no longer afraid of failure, when you are no longer concerned about what people will think, it will be easier for you to reach your goal.

If one plan doesn't work for you, make another plan. Too

many people give up too soon. Reevaluate your Mt. Everest. Is it really that high? Take another look. Is your dream to play the piano? Is your dream to be a painter and sell your paintings? Is your dream to accomplish something of value? Have you tried and failed? That doesn't make you a failure —it just means that it will take you longer to achieve your goal. If you permit the fear of failure to take hold of you, you will never accomplish anything—it will kill all your dreams. Try again, and again. Someone else's Mt. Everest may be just to conquer the cigarette habit or to lose thirty pounds. They, too, have to keep trying and trying, until one day they will finally succeed.

Do not permit anyone to deter you from your goal. You must save your energy. Don't drain it needlessly in frustration or anger. Keep your energy in your emotional bank account and use it for pleasure and accomplishment. Don't use it foolishly for worrying. Don't be a "hurrier"—do everything in a calm and relaxed manner. A person who is always rushing not only expends too much energy, but also looks awkward and does not exude charm. Learn to move smoothly and gracefully. You will look younger.

Be enthusiastic about realizing your dream. Enthusiasm is the starter. Laugh more. When it comes to enjoying life, there is no middle ground. Either you enjoy your life or you don't enjoy your life. "But I have so many problems," you may say. "How can I enjoy my life?" What do the external problems have to do with your ability to laugh at a joke, enjoy a good dinner, a good play, or good company? You can still enjoy your life while you are handling your problems or looking for solutions. I'm not saying to ignore your problems—that's not facing reality. You may not have control over certain external happenings, but you do have control over your reactions to those happenings. Here is an effective method to deal with any kind of a problem:

1. Define your problem—verbalize it. Some people don't know what their problem is. Is it a frustration that's getting you down? Is it a rejection? Have you been harboring a grudge for a long time? Are you bored? Keep digging until you become aware of what your real problem is.

2. You have a choice—you can evaluate your problem constructively or destructively. *How you think about your problem will be the deciding factor in how you will feel emotionally* and how you will continue to react. The choice is yours. You do not have to suffer; you do not have to be depressed; you do not have to be unhappy. Problems are a part of life, and if you work on changing what you can change in your life and accepting what you must accept, you will be healthier and happier. Some people just "mouth" acceptance of a situation. They say, "Of course, I accept my situation—what else can I do?" But they suffer from all kinds of psychosomatic symptoms. That's lip service, not acceptance—they are fooling themselves. If one *truly* accepts what he must accept, the person usually does not have psychological symptoms. That's the true test of acceptance.

Some people become frustrated or unhappy when it rains. That's an attitude—an irrational attitude. If it rains, it rains. You can't do anything about the weather, so why waste your good energy? What has the rain got to do with your happiness? Happiness comes from within. "Well," you may say, "it's frustrating, I planned a picnic." So you did. How about this thing called flexibility or this thing called adaptation? It's raining, so you think up another way to spend the day and get *fun* out of it. Teach your grandchildren flexibility—teach them to adapt to different circumstances when they visit you. Don't worry about leaving them great wealth—leave them the real values of life and they will be successful human beings. It's true that this is their parents' job, but if they spend a lot of time with you, you will be reinforcing these qualities.

Serenity doesn't come to you by pressing a button. It

comes from flexibility. If you can't do one thing, you do something else. You can't be licked if you refuse to be licked. You may have experienced despair, grief, illness, and perhaps you still haven't gotten over it. What are you doing about it? You must make a decision. Either you will muddle along with unhappiness for the rest of your life or choose to live a *new* life. Have faith in your ability to improve and grow; have faith in your capacity to stand up to your problems; have faith in your ability to climb your Mt. Everest. Say to yourself, "As of this moment, I am closing the door on yesterday and going forward to a new life." Say it with conviction, say it until your mind believes it, say it until it becomes a reality.

The best is yet to come. As long as you are alive you have the opportunity to find your own kind of happiness. Be in love with life—strive to enrich the best years of your life. And these *are* the best years. Most of your responsibilities are behind you. You have Bar Mitzvahs, Bat Mitzvahs, christenings, communions, confirmations, graduations, weddings, births of grandchildren to look forward to. Don't you think the best is yet to come? When I asked my classes, they said, "How can you say the best is yet to come at *our* age?" "Think about it all week," I answered, "and let me know next week if I'm out of my mind for making such a statement." The following week I could sense a change in attitude. Here are just a few remarks: "I thought about it all week, you're right. I'm going to my grandson's Bar Mitzvah in a few weeks and I realized that I don't have to do a damn thing. I'm a guest. I have no responsibility. My children have the headache now."

"I'm going to my granddaughter's wedding next month. I, too, have no responsibility. What a pleasure it is just to be a 'guest.' "

"I didn't realize that the best is yet to come. I didn't see it that way. I kept thinking only of my age and that life is almost over."

You can choose to take a negative attitude toward your advancing years or you can choose to take a positive attitude. If you choose to take a positive attitude—the best is yet to come.